SECRET
TAMPA BAY

A Guide to the Weird, Wonderful, and Obscure

Joshua Ginsberg

DEDICATION

In memory of my friend Steven, who was and
will always be a member of my party.
I have thus amended our childhood motto:
"No matter where I go, there we are."

CONTENTS

ACKNOWLEDGMENTS

While creating this book has been a labor of love, that is not, by any means, to suggest that I could have done it alone. Indeed, I have received far more assistance than I could have hoped for—so much so that to name every individual and source who contributed to *Secret Tampa Bay* would vastly exceed the space I have here. That said, there are some without whom this book could not exist, and as such are worthy of special recognition here.

First, there is my wife Jennifer, who has been not just my partner on countless adventures, but my own personal Polaris—a single, fixed point of light that guides my way home. She has faced down fear of clowns, reptiles, and open fires and has patiently waited while I inspected every last Fiji mermaid and read every historical marker along every path we've traveled. We are joined by Tinker Bell the Shih Tzu, who is as fierce a protector and loyal a companion as any human could wish for. I also want to thank our family—Andy and Bob, David and Myrna, Debbie and Howard, Barbara and Jon, Ali, Jeremy, Seth, and Adam. I am thankful every day for your love and support.

There are many friends and colleagues who have contributed either directly or indirectly to this work. Thanks are owed to Candi and Tom for your friendship and continually superior recommendations regarding local sites; to Dwight Peterson whose friendship and insight has made me a better and more thoughtful writer and human being; to Gary Silber, Mehul Soni, and Jacob Gehl for reviewing some of the early versions of this book; to my gifted colleagues Mark Sutz and Mary Dismore at Your Signature Resume; to Larry Hayward, Jason "Venture Monkey" Ewing, Bobby Conway and Ayesha Hamid; to the Pirates of Maddness (my GISH team) for the annual week-long dose of creative absurdity; and to all current and former members of the Studio at Grant Thornton—by far the most talented and compassionate group of proposal writers I have ever had the privilege of calling coworkers.

I am also profoundly grateful to everyone at Reedy Press including Josh Stevens, Barbara Northcott, Laura Slown, Don Korte, and all of the copy editors and design staff for their expertise and guidance in transforming my sometimes marginally intelligible collection of vignettes into the cogent and polished finished product you see here. My thanks also extend to fellow Reedy Press authors such as Kristin Hare, who very generously shared her time and insight with me.

A great many individuals kindly opened their doors to me and helped make sure I got my facts straight. This includes the inimitable Joy Rose, Christine Thompson, and Bobby Vandercar; the Tampa Bay Ale Trail team; Jim Oleson, John Perodeau, Dennis Schrader, and Stephen Jones at the Replay Museum; Brian Schmit at the Rao Musunuru M.D. Museum; the kind folks of the Marion County Parks & Recreation; the Movement Sanctuary team; the tour guides at Florida CraftArt, Tampa Mafia Tour, Ybor City Ghost Tour and Tabanero Cigars; and all of the many knowledgeable curators, historians, and staff at the Henry B. Plant Museum, the West Pasco Historical Society, the Tampa Bay History Center, the James Museum of Western & Wildlife Art, the Dunedin Historical Society, Mote Marine Laboratory & Aquarium, the St. Petersburg Museum of History, and the Dali Museum, among others.

I am also indebted to those I met along the way who are blazing inspiring paths of their own; those urban explorers, writers, researchers, and seekers of wonder such as Dylan Thuras and the folks at Atlas Obscura, Adam Selzer at Mysterious Chicago, and the people behind Abandoned Florida, Weird U.S., Roadside America, and similar resources. Thank you to Dunkin Donuts for all of the iced black coffee (with the sugar free French vanilla flavor) and to the band Lord Huron for providing the ideal soundtrack for exploring Florida's strange trails.

INTRODUCTION

How much do you really know about the place you live?

It's the sort of question you might ask when you first move somewhere new, but over time you probably find yourself asking it less often, if at all. However amazing the place you call home, be it an urban condo, a rural farmhouse, a tent in the desert, or a traveling circus sideshow train car, inevitably all the wonders around you seem to fade into the background against which you live your daily life. That was the case for me, anyhow. After 10 years in Chicago I had gone blind to the city's magic, and it took the unexpected loss of one of my closest friends to snap me out of my routine trance.

After consideration, my wife and I agreed that we didn't want to spend forever in the same place. Before moving, we decided to use our last few months really exploring and learning all we could about the city we were leaving. That's when I first discovered resources like the guidebooks produced by Reedy Press.

Upon arriving in Tampa, I committed myself to preserving that sense of curiosity that comes with a new environment. Nearly four years in, I think I've done a pretty good job. It helps that my wife and my four-legged companion, Tinker Bell, are willing to join me in my adventures, even if it means stopping at every single historical marker along the way.

Whether you're a resident or a visitor in the Tampa Bay area, I sincerely hope that you will enjoy experiencing the unusual sites and activities in this book as much as I have enjoyed writing about them.

Okay, that's all I have to say. So, without further ado, let's get to it because we've got a whole lot to cover.

THE STORY OF TAMPA

Can you learn the history of a city from one painting?

From the Pensacola graffiti bridge to Miami's Wynwood walls to the St. Petersburg murals, Florida isn't shy about promoting its public artwork. Tampa has several notable paintings, sculptures, and other creative works, but one of its most historically focused is hiding quietly on the lobby wall of a municipal building on Jackson Street.

Artist Lynn Ash was commissioned in 2003 by the City of Tampa's Public Art Program to create a large painting incorporating as much of the unique character and history of the city as possible. The result was a collage of more than 100 mini-paintings that include portraits of prominent local figures and scenes that capture Tampa's shining achievements.

Just a few of the highlights include the area's indigenous people, de Soto's exploration, Tony Jannus' historic flight, the fictional pirate Gasparilla, the opening of MacDill Air Force Base, the establishment of Columbia

A PICTURE IS WORTH A THOUSAND WORDS

What: The Story of Tampa (4' x 8' acrylic painting on Masonite)

Where: Lobby of the Tampa Municipal Office Building, 306 E. Jackson St., Tampa

Cost: Free

Pro Tip: If you like the artwork, ask for a print and a brochure that includes a key to the various images. Staff at the front desk usually keep some for visitors.

Artist Lynn Ash was employed at Busch Gardens, where you can see some of his artworks. If you have keen eyes, you can find a wishbone hidden in each of his paintings.

Lynn Ash's artwork is an extraordinary, if little known, visual history of the Tampa Bay area.

Restaurant in Ybor, pro golfer Mildred "Babe" Didrikson Zaharias (who was named Greatest Female Athlete of the First Half of the 20th Century), the opening of the Florida Aquarium, and the Buccaneers' Super Bowl XXXVII victory. Portraits include political figures such as Joseph Lancaster (Tampa's first mayor) and José Martí; businessmen like Henry Plant, Vicente Martinez-Ybor, and Moses White; baseball greats Al López and Babe Ruth; and Tampa's first poet laureate, James E. Tokley, to name just a few.

If that weren't enough, around the edge of the painting are smaller frames depicting some of the native flora and fauna.

You can find a key to all the mini-paintings on the Tampa Public Art website, but it's worth testing your local knowledge by first seeing how many you can identify on your own.

THE MOST CELEBRATED PIRATE WHO PROBABLY NEVER LIVED

Who is Gasparilla and why is his name attached to everything?

Fictional pirates like Jack Sparrow and Long John Silver may be better known worldwide, but it's Gasparilla who gets his own festival in Tampa each year.

The gist of the story is that José Gaspar was born into Spanish nobility in the mid- to late 1700s and served in the royal navy. One version has him framed, disgraced, and unjustly banished to sea for an affair with a young woman at court. Other variations paint him as a mutineer or cunning crown jewel thief. What all the stories agree upon is that eventually he turned to piracy under the name Gasparilla and took special pleasure in sending to the bottom of the sea the same Spanish galleons upon which he once served.

After 40 years of terrorizing Tampa Bay, Gaspar decided to retire. However, he and his crew couldn't resist one last opportunity when they spotted what appeared to be a distressed British merchant ship. It turned out to be an ambush, and out from hiding came the famed pirate-hunting USS Enterprise, which made short work of Gasparilla's own ship. Before the pirate captain was captured, he is said to have wrapped himself in the anchor chains and shouted, "No one will ever take Gasparilla alive," before plunging overboard to his watery grave.

The Children's Gasparilla Parade is a family-friendly version that takes place the week before the official invasion.

4

Gasparilla is essentially a "Pirate Mardi Gras," complete with beads, floats, and parades.

PIRATES ON PARADE

What: Gasparilla Pirate Festival

Where: All along Bayshore Boulevard and into Ybor City

Cost: Free

Pro Tip: Plan as if you were attending Mardi Gras or New Year's Eve in Times Square—it will get crowded quickly, parking will be scarce, and if you want a prime sport for viewing the floats or catching beads, you'll want to show up early.

Despite cannonball-sized holes in the story, the legend has endured. In 1904 Ye Mystic Krewe of Gasparilla was established as part of the May Day festival. It has since evolved into a weeklong celebration which begins the last Saturday in January of each year, when pirates sail across Tampa Bay, seize the key to the city, and then parade down Bayshore Boulevard.

CITY WITHIN A CITY

How do you pronounce Ybor?

Ybor (pronounced EE-bor) City is the historic neighborhood that gave Tampa its signature Cuban sandwich and the nickname "Cigar City." Founded as his own company town in the 1880s by cigar manufacturer Vicente Martinez-Ybor, who was looking to relocate his operations from Key West, the neighborhood is noteworthy for a variety of reasons. For one thing, it was a prosperous city unto itself, built and populated almost entirely by immigrants. Initially, this meant primarily Cubans and Spaniards, followed by Italians and Eastern European Jews, who brought their culture, cuisine, and mutual aid societies. Another unusual feature was that Ybor City operated essentially outside the laws of the rest of Tampa, governed by Ybor himself (very much like Chicago's Pullman District). Here, Ybor built homes, a streetcar line, Tampa's first brewery, and a great many other businesses.

Ybor City thrived up until the Great Depression, which, coupled with automation,

KEEPING YBOR WEIRD

What: Ybor City

Where: E. 7th Ave., Tampa

Cost: Free to wander and window shop. Admission to the Ybor City Museum is $4 per person; free for children ages 5 and under.

Pro Tip: Where there is gentrification, there is often friction. Take appropriate precautions and always be cognizant of your surroundings.

The wonders of Ybor City are numerous—a good place to begin is with a visit to the Ybor City Museum and tour of a typical cigar worker's casita.

Eighth Avenue is Ybor City's main street for bars and restaurants, cigar shops, tattoo parlors, and unique shops

shuttered virtually all of the cigar factories. Sensing a profit in the illegal bolita lottery game, organized crime moved into the area and brought with it political corruption, bootlegging, prostitution, and other forms of vice. Thus began Ybor City's long decline, which would continue despite multiple urban renewal efforts until the early 1990s.

Today Ybor is once again a prime destination for both tourists and locals. While it has evolved to keep pace with the time and trends, it fiercely maintains its distinctive character.

DELVING DEEPER INTO YBOR

What else makes Ybor unlike the rest of Tampa Bay?

Ybor has undergone substantial renewal over the past several years, but all throughout the neighborhood, hiding just under the surface, are reminders of its dark past.

To start with, in 1908, the largest fire in Tampa's history began at 1914 12th St., consuming more than 17 city blocks and an unknown number of human lives. Some claim that they can still hear the voices and laughter of the children who perished in the blaze.

Then there's the Cuban Club. Despite its architectural beauty, its propensity for tragedy has landed it on the Travel Channel's list of the Top 10 Most Haunted Places. Some of the spirits alleged to reside there include a shamed actor who killed himself on the stage of the theater, a former board member who was murdered by another during a heated argument, and Jimmy, an 8-year-old boy who drowned in the indoor pool on the lower level.

Across from the Cuban Club is the former Don Vicente de Ybor Historic Inn, which served as a public health clinic for its first 70 years. The ghost of a nurse who worked there is said to still roam the halls, and a mad doctor is rumored to have used the basement incinerator there to dispose of up to a dozen of his failed experiments in reanimating the dead.

The plot thickens: more than a few conspiracy theorists believe that the plan to assassinate President Kennedy was hatched around a table in Ybor City by prominent members of the Cigar City Mafia.

Stained-glass windows, ornate design, and numerous tragedies make the phase "hauntingly beautiful" an apt description of Ybor City's Cuban Club.

What would make Ybor even stranger than all the hauntings? How about a network of underground tunnels? Most likely built as sewers, they were put to more nefarious use by smugglers, bootleggers, and human traffickers. Access to the tunnels has been sealed off for good reason—after more than a century of neglect, the slightest motion can be enough to trigger a collapse.

BENEATH THE SURFACE

What: Ybor City's haunted and hidden history

Where: Throughout Ybor City

Cost: Free to roam on your own. The Ybor City Ghost Tour price is adults, $25; children, $10.

Pro Tip: Even if you manage to find an opening, under no circumstances should you go exploring the tunnels.

FLORIDA'S FIRST MAGIC KINGDOM

Why does that University of Tampa building have domes topped with crescents?

February 5, 1891, was a momentous day in the history of Tampa—it marked the opening of railroad magnate Henry Bradley Plant's Tampa Bay Hotel, and with it the city's transformation from a minor stop to a major travel destination. Designed by architect J. A. Wood, the hotel was the first on Florida's west coast to have electric lights and telephones, as well as the first working elevator—it still functions today, making it one of the oldest continually operating elevators in the nation. The building was said to be fireproof, owing to its concrete and steel-reinforced structure.

In total, 21 buildings occupied the 150 acres of hotel grounds, along with a racetrack, golf course, swimming pool, and bowling

FIT FOR A RAILROAD TYCOON

What: Henry B. Plant Museum

Where: 401 W. Kennedy Blvd., Tampa

Cost: Adults, $10; seniors and students, $7; children ages 4–12, $5; children ages 3 and under, free

Pro Tip: If you're visiting in December, check out the annual Victorian Christmas Stroll, which includes complementary hot cider and caroling.

Henry Plant's story mirrors that of Henry Flagler—both men built railroad empires along Florida's coasts, both built magnificent hotels which became educational institutions, and both are said to still haunt the palaces they built.

Each December the museum gets a Victorian Christmas makeover.

alley. The six minarets, four cupolas, and three domes reflected the Moorish Revival style that was popular at the time among those Plant anticipated would occupy the 511 rooms (and take his trains when arriving and departing, of course). Over the years, celebrity visitors included the Prince of Wales, Stephen Crane, Winston Churchill, Clara Barton, and Sarah Bernhardt. But few visitors were more celebrated than Colonel Teddy Roosevelt, who led the Rough Riders and used Plant's hotel as the US military's base of operations during the Spanish–American War.

The hotel closed during the Great Depression but found new life as classrooms for Tampa Junior College, which eventually evolved into the University of Tampa. The Tampa Municipal Museum in the South Wing of the estate, which was renamed the Henry B. Plant Museum in 1974, continues to preserve the hotel's history, original furnishings, artifacts, and legacy.

EXTRA CREDIT

Who was Roger Babson and why did he hate gravity?

If you have some time before or after visiting the Henry B. Plant Museum, take a stroll around the University of Tampa campus, where you can find several memorable and unusual monuments and markers.

The first marker you're likely to notice is that of "Babe's Longest Homer." Where the John H. Sykes College of Business stands today was once the site of Tampa's downtown stadium, Plant Field. And it was here on April 4, 1919, in a game between the New York Giants and the Boston Red Sox, that Babe Ruth hit the ball 587 feet for the longest home run of his career.

Around the corner from Babe's longest home run is the "Anti-Gravity Rock." The University of Tampa is home to one of the 15 gravity research monuments on various college campuses throughout the eastern United States. Founded in 1948 by wealthy business man Roger Babson—who was also a presidential candidate, prolific author, and friend of Thomas Edison—the Gravity Research Foundation was Babson's tool in his quest to defeat gravity, which he blamed for the drowning deaths of his sister and grandson. According to the inscription on the stone, it was erected in 1965 "to remind students of the blessings forthcoming when

---

Although the plaque states that the cannon is from Fort Dade, that's technically not correct. The original cannon was donated for steel scrap during World War II and later replaced with a cannon of similar vintage from Fort Morgan, Alabama.

BABE'S LONGEST HOMER

At Tampa's Plant Field on April 4, 1919, "Babe" Ruth, playing for the Boston Red Sox against the N.Y. Giants, smacked a 587-foot home run that set a record in a pre-season game. 4,300 screaming fans saw the feat. Famed Evangelist Billy Sunday, an ex-major leaguer himself, who was conducting a tent revival on the Florida Fair grounds nearby, had pitched the first ball of the game, and The Bambino's pace-setting ball was presented to him. Ruth played from 1915 to 1935. He is regarded as the most popular player and greatest slugger in history. One year he hit 60 homers.

ERECTED 1961 BY THE TAMPA HISTORICAL SOCIETY IN COOPERATION WITH THE ITALIAN-AMERICAN GOLF ASSOCIATION, INC.

JOHN H. SYKES COLLEGE OF BUSINESS

The longest home run of Babe Ruth's career is memorialized next to the John H. Sykes College of Business.

science determines what gravity is, how it works and how it may be controlled."

Also worth mentioning is the De Soto Oak, under which the explorer is said to have made peace with local tribes; the iconic *Sticks of Fire* sculpture, a visual interpretation of the Calusa word *tanpa*, from which the city takes its name; and the Spanish–American War Memorial, atop which sits a gigantic, Cuba-facing artillery cannon.

LONG SHOTS AND HEAVY CONCEPTS

What: Multiple monuments and markers

Where: University of Tampa and Plant Park, Tampa

Cost: Free

Pro Tip: You can pick up a parking pass if you're visiting the Plant Museum.

CRACKER COUNTRY

Isn't it kind of inappropriate to call someone a Cracker?

Before we talk about the 13 original structures that Mildred and Doyle Carlton Jr. collected and rebuilt adjacent to the Florida State Fairgrounds, we should review the term *cracker*. It dates at least as far back as Shakespearean times and was used around 1900 to describe the self-reliant and often poor American pioneers who migrated south. They became known as "Florida Crackers," due to their use of whips in hunting and herding cattle that had been let loose by the Spaniards. Today, cracker is more often an ethnic slur for caucasians of Northern European decent, synonymous with "white trash."

That said, we can turn our attention to the living history museum established in 1978 for the preservation and interpretation of rural life in Florida in the late 19th century. Original structures, which have been collected from throughout the state and painstakingly restored, include the Okahumpka Train Depot, built in 1898 and now home to a massive model train layout of the region; wooden caboose #0583 from the Atlantic Coast Line Railroad; the Governors Inn, a 1912 structure originally from Lily; the Carlton House, built in 1885 and the birthplace of Florida's Depression-era governor; and the Rainey Store, built in the 1880s in Ona. There's

---

In the post office you might see a wanted poster for John Ashley. Known as the "King of the Everglades," Ashley was a bootlegger, bank robber, and occasional pirate who achieved folk hero status—essentially a swampland John Dillinger.

14

The Cracker County General Store is one of 13 authentic old Florida buildings rebuilt and preserved at the site.

also an 1880s print shop where you can pick up the mock daily news, a schoolhouse, a corn crib, a post office, and a church.

All of these buildings are staffed with volunteers and docents in period attire, ready to regale you with stories of Southern pioneer life, teach you to tie advanced knots, and serenade you with their banjos, fiddles, and mountain dulcimers.

BUILT TO LAST

What: Cracker Country

Where: 4800 US Hwy. 301 N., Tampa

Cost: Free

Pro Tip: Cracker Country is only open to the public for a total of two weeks each year. If you miss it, you can see similarly collected and restored buildings at both Heritage Village and the Pioneer Florida Museum.

SHINE ON

How does a city prevent graffiti artists from tagging the walls of vacant buildings?

Like many cities and towns throughout Florida around 2008, St. Petersburg had a problem. With developers making big promises just a year earlier, many commercial property owners had taken pains to remove older, lower-paying business tenants from their properties, but once the market soured, the city was left with a glut of vacant properties. This in turn attracted vandalism—especially graffiti—which added insult to economic injury.

With a wealth of local creative talent, a few forward-thinking property owners decided to try an innovative tactic—namely, hiring local street artists to create massive artworks on the exteriors of their buildings. Out of respect, generally speaking, other would-be "muralists" ceased leaving their tags over the artwork of others.

The concept worked so well that artists Leon Bedore, better known as Tes One, and Chris Parks, aka Palehorse, decided to

MOVE OVER, BANKSY

What: SHINE St. Pete Mural Festival

Where: Downtown St. Petersburg

Cost: Free to wander and watch artists at work. The Saturday morning walking tour provided through Florida CraftArt costs $19 for adults, $11 for children ages 6–18, and is free for children ages 5 and under.

Pro Tip: You can find an interactive map at www.stpetemuraltour.com/map-of-st-pete-murals.

Cecilia Lueza chose a more literal interpretation of "street art"—her work covers the intersection at 501 Central Ave.

16

Chad Mize's mural of a starry-eyed Twiggy is a perennial local favorite.

organize the first SHINE St. Pete Mural Festival in 2015. They invited emerging, established, and respected artists to come and leave their own distinct and impressive creative marks on the city. The first year drew talent from throughout Florida, as well as New York (Morning Breath and Erik Jones), California (Ricky Watts and Shark Toof), and Rome, Italy (Hitnes). A seed grant was provided by the City of St. Petersburg's Office of Cultural Affairs with matching donations from the St. Petersburg Arts Alliance (SPAA), who now produces the event.

Every year the level of talent and the scope of projects has increased, creating a vibrant downtown art scene, as well as a lucrative tourist attraction. While the mural festival occurs in mid-October each year, you'll find new artworks popping up all year long. Florida CraftArt offers "The Official St. Pete Walking Mural Tour," which provides an excellent introduction and overview, and there are also Arts District Mural Tours by Bicycle if you want to cover more ground.

ROOFTOP ODDITIES

What exactly is that doing way up there?

With so much to see in the Tampa Bay area, it can be easy to forget that the nearest wonder might be just overhead.

For one thing, there's the glistening metal dragon that watches the traffic along Kennedy Avenue from her perch atop Associated Watch & Jewelry. That would be Daenerys, and at roughly 40 feet in length, she is indeed the mother of dragons. Owner Kevin Burns first saw her belching flame from a floating platform at a dragon boat race and decided to break her chains and bring her home. He installed her on the roof of his store but had to disable her fire-breathing capabilities for insurance reasons. When she was taken down temporarily for maintenance, Burns discovered that she had been pointing in the wrong direction. Since correcting this feng shui faux pas, he has noticed an increase in business.

Passing by 2309 N. Dale Mabry Hwy., the casual observer might think that aliens have landed on a local strip club. The "UFO" on the roof of the building is actually an example of the rare "Futuro House," a concept created in the 1960s by Finnish athlete turned architect Matti Suuronen. Although the Futuro House never gained mainstream acceptance, this particular one has found a new purpose as the VIP room of the strip club 2001 Odyssey.

Taking I-275 into St. Petersburg, you might see another gargantuan rooftop reptile snatching a fly out of the sky.

Tampa isn't the only place in Florida where you can find a Futuro House—there's one in Pensacola Beach that serves as the headquarters of the city's historical society.

If you didn't know any better, you might think that aliens have landed in search of a good time.

Composed from car parts, *Security Lizard* may be the best known of sculptor Paul Eppling's creative metalworks, and it sits, appropriately, over St. Pete's police car garage. Although Eppling died in 2016, many of his works are still lurking in unexpected places throughout the Tampa Bay area.

A DIFFERENT PERSPECTIVE

What: Various rooftop creations

Where: Throughout Tampa Bay

Cost: Free to view from outside. If you want to see the interior of the strip club UFO, it will cost you $200 for 15 minutes.

Pro Tip: If you're going to be staring skyward, keep a pair of sunglasses handy.

SHELTER FROM THE STORM

Is Tampa Bay protected from the elements by ancient Tocobaga magic?

Thousands of years ago Tampa Bay was home to the Weeden Island Cultures, and later the Calusa and Tocobaga. These early Florida natives left behind artifacts, wooden canoes, and earthworks in the form of shell middens and burial/temple mounds. While many of these have been lost to development (including at least a half dozen in St. Petersburg and one where the Tampa Convention Center now stands), there are still plenty of others you can visit today. Of those, historians believe the Safety Harbor Mound inside Philippe Park is the most significant, as it may have been the capital of the Tocobaga civilization.

There are legends of a Tocobaga shaman who secured the area from storms by ascending this mound at sunset each night. From there he would call upon the spirit of the land to defend against storms and floods. Odet Philippe himself is said to have survived the hurricane of 1848 by climbing to the top of the mound at the edge of his land. Once the storm passed, Philippe observed devastation all around him, but he and the mound he had sheltered on were miraculously unscathed.

Tampa's history of dodging catastrophic storms is indeed notable—prior to Irma, the last major hurricane to hit the area was in 1928—but there are plenty of less mystical explanations for this.

While his connection to Napoleon has been largely debunked, Odet Philippe is credited as the first European settler in Pinellas County, the first to cultivate grapefruit in Florida, and the first to introduce cigar-making to Tampa.

Near the mound is a grave marker for Odet Philippe, but the exact location of his remains is unknown.

HIGHER GROUND

What: Philippe Park

Where: 2525 Philippe Pkwy., Safety Harbor

Cost: Free

Pro Tip: If you're willing to travel a bit further north, Crystal River Archaeological State Park offers a unique "Moon over the Mounds" series of guided walking tours—check the park's website for dates and additional information.

Storms moving west across the state tend to lose power over land, and the rare storms that come up the Gulf Coast are often carried north past Tampa. All the same, there are more than a few locals who claim to have seen a shadowy figure climb to the top of the mound at sunset before disappearing like a wisp of smoke.

PURVEYORS OF THE PECULIAR

Where might a coven go to restock its spell components? (Just asking for a friend.)

If "your friend" is in the market for bat wings, beetle carapaces, Ouija boards, or even more macabre offerings, there's more than one local source for such goods.

Dysfunctional Grace Art Co. is a good first stop. True to its claim as "the only shop in Ybor City where death and dysfunction dance in a graceful ballet," you will find a vast assortment of items here with an emphasis on celebrating life by embracing and elevating its inevitable end to a form of art. From antique surgical instruments to ceremonial daggers to taxidermy artwork with a steampunk twist and all manner of preserved flora and fauna, you are certain to find that missing something for your Victorian cabinet of curiosities. Be prepared though—you may encounter something here that will evoke a strong reaction, such as fear, joy, revulsion, fascination, or maybe all of these simultaneously. Whatever it is that you feel, just keep in mind that the proprietors take pains to ensure that everything displayed was acquired and preserved ethically and respectfully.

If you can't find what you're seeking at Dysfunctional Grace, fear not—another equally wondrous and unsettling shopping experience

---

For something more fluffy than frightening, check out La France in Ybor City or Peaches and Pearls in Westchase. On the other hand, if you need to own something that looks like it clawed its way out of a nightmare, seek out local artist Juan Cabana.

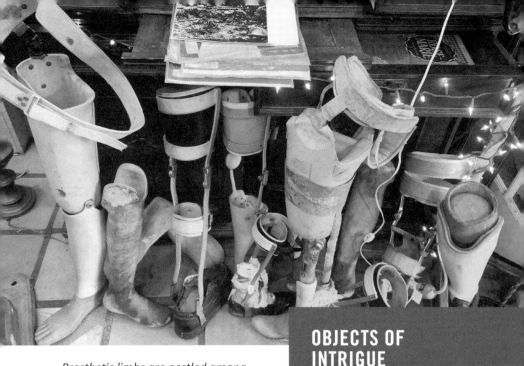

Prosthetic limbs are nestled among other medical, scientific, and pseudo-scientific supplies at Oddities and Antiques.

OBJECTS OF INTRIGUE

What: Unusual shopping experiences

Where: Multiple locations

Cost: Prices vary

Pro Tip: Should you find that you've brought home something more than you bargained for, there are plenty of online resources regarding the proper handling of cursed objects.

awaits you in Clearwater at Oddities and Antiques. In addition to the owner's own metal artwork displayed throughout the store, you will find a truly unique collection. A short list of what can be procured here includes Erlenmeyer flasks, Civil War bullets, plague doctor masks, DIY exorcism kits, chainmail armor, chastity belts, and a petrified dinosaur egg. If you don't mind paying an arm and a leg, you can take home a dozen of each from their wide selection of prosthetic limbs.

Just think, many of these rare and one-of-a-kind items could be equally at home in a museum, a medieval torture chamber . . . or your living room!

VISIONS OF KEROUAC

Where and how did the king of the beats spend his final years?

Long before St. Petersburg became a mecca for hipsters, it was the final home of the original cool cat, Jack Kerouac. Born in Lowell, MA, the Beat Generation front man and *On the Road* author's last abode was on 10th Avenue, where he lived with his mother, Gabrielle, and his third wife, Stella, from 1966 to 1969.

Well known for his booze- and Benzedrine-fueled adventures with his literary brethren, his time in the Sunshine City was marked by both internal and external conflict. He spent many nights on a cot in his backyard under the stars in search of his own Buddhist nirvana, but just as often he succumbed to his demons, which brought him to the neighborhood bar, the Flamingo, for a shot of whiskey and a wash of beer. By day he would work on stories or roam the aisles of Haslam's bookstore, bringing stacks of his own works up to the front to give them more prominence.

Kerouac's external conflicts with his neighbors culminated in a particularly brutal bar fight just weeks before he was rushed to St. Anthony's Hospital after vomiting blood from an esophageal hemorrhage. He died at the hospital at 5:15 a.m. on October 21, 1969, and while the official cause of death was listed as cirrhosis, many suspect that the injuries he sustained in his last brawl hastened his demise.

For a short time, from 1957 to 1958, Kerouac lived in Orlando at 1418 Clouser Ave., which now provides residencies for authors through the Kerouac Project of Orlando.

Kerouac's favorite local waterhole has become a shrine to the late Beat Generation author.

The author's former home was sold in June of 2020, but the Flamingo Sports Bar has survived and become a shrine of sorts, with a large mural on the outside wall and "a shot and a wash" on the menu.

THE BEAT GOES ON

What: Jack Kerouac's regular bar in St. Petersburg

Where: Kerouac's home was 5169 10th Ave. N. The Flamingo Sports Bar is located at 1230 9th St. N., St. Petersburg

Cost: A shot and a wash at the Flamingo will cost you a mere $2.25.

Pro Tip: If you find the smell of cigarette smoke overpowering, you can get some fresh air outside on the patio area.

GARDENS GONE WILD

What happens when a private garden blossoms into an unexpected roadside attraction?

Tampa's hot, humid summers and mild, dry winters make it perfect for year-round fishing, baseball, and, of course, gardening. Consequently, you'll find extraordinary gardens in seemingly every neighborhood throughout the city, but some of these, like the Sunken Gardens, deserve special mention.

In 1903, when plumber George Turner purchased six acres of land and drained a lake on his property to create his own garden, he probably didn't expect that a century later his work would achieve perennial popularity as St. Petersburg's oldest "living museum" and one of America's oldest roadside attractions. Turner laid an elaborate, winding path through his neighborhood jungle, creating the illusion of far greater space than it actually occupies. The rich soil at the bottom of the lake (which makes it below sea level) proved perfect for cultivation, starting with some citrus trees and vegetables.

As his garden expanded to include a nursery with fresh fruit and vegetables, neighbors began dropping in and, by the 1920s, Turner was charging a nickel for tours. When George passed away in 1961, his sons took over and acquired the adjacent Sanitary Public Market building, converting it for a time into the World's Largest

---

There's a local legend about the fossilized limestone rock found at the center of the sinkhole lake when it was drained. Named the Growing Stone, it is said to grant inner harmony, tranquility, and a talent for making things grow to any who sit upon it.

It doesn't get more vintage roadside attraction than the sign out front of Sunken Gardens.

ENCHANTED

What: Sunken Gardens

Where: 1825 4th St. N., St. Petersburg

Cost: Adults, $10; seniors, $8; children ages 11 and under, $4

Pro Tip: Sunken Gardens is a very popular wedding spot, so try not to photobomb someone's special day, and hands off the cake and champagne.

Gift Shop and the King of Kings Wax Museum. Ownership passed to their children, who continued to operate the garden until 1999, when the city of St. Petersburg acquired it.

Today the Sunken Gardens include a Japanese Garden, Cactus Garden, and Butterfly Garden, as well as fauna such as koi, tortoises, and a flock of Chilean flamingoes. Educational programs, tours, and special events are offered regularly at this verdant marvel that's rooted as deeply in St. Petersburg's history as in its soil.

SAFETY HARBOR'S OLDEST RESIDENT

Is there a living organism in Safety Harbor that's more than three centuries old?

Safety Harbor has seen plenty of human beings come and go over the years. For thousands of years there were tribes of indigenous people. In 1539 Hernando de Soto arrived, thinking that he might have stumbled upon the fabled fountain of youth. Then there was Colonel W. J. Bailey, who was the first owner of the springs under the flag of the United States. The next owner, Captain James F. Tucker, built the Safety Harbor Sanatorium there in 1920. Dr. Alben Jansik restored the resort in 1936, and Dr. Salem Baranoff acquired the land in 1945 to establish a resort health spa.

And all the while, one massive oak tree continued uninterested and uninterrupted, sprouting along at a steady pace of 12 inches per year. The Baranoff Oak, as it's now called, has a trunk diameter of about 20 feet and weighs roughly 800 tons, with concrete pillars to support its monstrous limbs. It has been on the historic registry of live oaks since 1934 and is estimated to be 350 to 500 years old, making it quite possibly the oldest living thing in all of Pinellas County.

The oldest known tree in Florida was "the Senator" of Longwood—a 3,500-year-old bald cypress, until it met a fiery end in 2012. The individual who accidentally started the fire was quoted as saying, "I can't believe I burned down a tree older than Jesus."

The gentle giant known as the Baranoff Oak is a living local landmark.

GNARLY

What: The Baranoff Oak

Where: 101 2nd Ave. N., Safety Harbor

Cost: Free to view, $1M to own

Pro Tip: See it while you can.

The property that the oak sits on today is owned not by the city but rather by UCITA Properties, which entered into a 20-year deal back in 2002 to maintain and protect the tree. That deal expires in 2022, and at the time of this writing, the future of the great oak is uncertain. If the city fails to raise one million dollars to acquire the land, UCITA has expressed interest in expanding its current facility—which means that the safety of Safety Harbor's most senior resident is now threatened, ironically, by the need for more senior housing.

A MAJOR LEAGUE COLLECTION

What did baseballs look like back in the 1880s and how were they made?

In a place where summer lasts essentially all year long, a love affair with baseball was well-nigh inevitable. Tropicana Field is where you'll find hometown heroes the Tampa Bay Rays, but you can also catch minor league and spring training games for more than a dozen other teams. Predictably, you'll also find plenty of memorabilia around town celebrating "America's National Pastime."

Among collections of baseball memorabilia, Schrader's Little Cooperstown inside the St. Petersburg Museum of History is in a league of its own. As of this writing, the collection comprises 4,999 autographed baseballs spanning over 100 years of history. Recognized by the *Guinness Book of World Records* as the largest collection of signed baseballs in the world, it all began in 1956 at a Yankees' spring training game when a nine-year-old Dennis Schrader caught the eye of Mickey Mantle, who came over and signed the baseball he was holding.

You'll find the John Hancock of all the big-name hall of famers here: Babe Ruth, Ty Cobb, Joe DiMaggio, Shoeless Joe Jackson, and others. Schrader's collection covers all the bases, with special sections highlighting the All-American Girls Professional Baseball League,

---

Cooperstown, from which the collection gets its name, is the site of the Baseball Hall of Fame. Contrary to popular belief, however, the game was probably not invented there by Union Army officer Abner Doubleday in 1839.

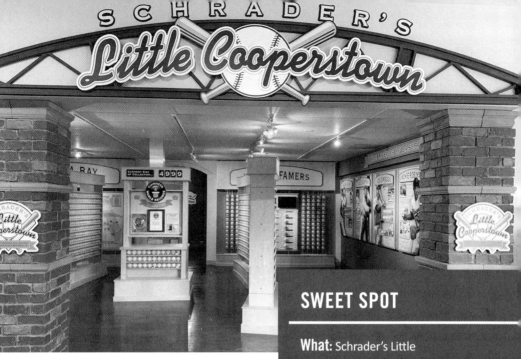

Baseball fans and autograph collectors will find that their passions intersect at Schrader's Little Cooperstown.

famous sportscasters, the Negro leagues, celebrities, and historical figures. A few highlights include multiple American presidents, the oldest survivor of the *Titanic*, Muhammad Ali, and a ball signed by both Amelia Earhart and Charles Lindbergh.

You could spend an entire day just reading the names in Schrader's collection, but don't miss some of the museum's other treasures, including a replica of the Benoist airplane made famous by Tony Jannus and a 3,000-year-old mummy known as "Our Lady of the Nile."

SWEET SPOT

What: Schrader's Little Cooperstown

Where: St. Petersburg Museum of History, 335 Second Ave. NE, St. Petersburg

Cost: Adults, $15; seniors, $12; military, veterans, students, teachers, and children ages 7–17, $9; children ages 6 and under, free

Pro Tip: Don't let size fool you—as the oldest museum in Pinellas County, what the St. Petersburg Museum of History lacks in square footage, it more than compensates for in content and quality.

FOREIGN SOIL

Is there a small part of Tampa that's owned by another country?

That Tampa, and more specifically Ybor City, has a close connection with Cuba is well known and evidenced by the multiple busts and statues to Cuban revolutionary and national hero José Martí. What many folks don't realize is just how physically close the connection is—so near, in fact, that you can actually stand on Cuban soil without taking a boat or plane.

Welcome to Parque Amigos de José Martí, which was donated to the Republic of Cuba in 1956 during the Batista administration. Despite the change in Cuban government just three years later when Castro came to power, and clashes between pro-Castro and anti-Castro groups throughout the 1960s, the park has remained the property of Cuba to this day. Maintenance and upkeep have been handled by the Cuban Historical and Cultural Center since 1990.

Within this miniature slice of Cuba, visitors will find soil transplanted from each of the Cuban provinces, a small mural of the Island of Cuba, and a statue of the park's namesake, José Julián Martí y Pérez, flanked by US and Cuban flags. Martí was a frequent visitor to Tampa, which he called *El Pueblo Fiel* ("the Faithful Town"), often speaking to crowds of Cuban cigar factory workers. The park itself is located on the former site of Paulina Pedroso's boarding

---

You may be joined at the park by some of Ybor City's most protected residents: feral chickens, which have roamed the neighborhood for over a century and will continue to do so for the foreseeable future, per a 2018 city council decision.

The only place in Tampa where you can stand on Cuban soil without leaving the country.

CUBA LIBRE

What: Parque Amigos de José Martí

Where: At the corner of E. Eighth Ave. and N. 13th St., Tampa

Cost: Free

Pro Tip: Hours can vary, but generally the park is open Monday through Friday from 8 a.m. to 1:30 p.m.

house, where she assisted Martí in recovering from a would-be assassin's poison.

Martí isn't the only hero of Cuban independence to have a statue in the park. Visitors will also find a bust of Antonio Maceo Grajales, who rose to the rank of major general during the Ten Years' War, part of Cuba's fight for independence, and led the invasion of Cuba from Oriente Province in 1896.

HOOKED ON LIVE MERMAID SHOWS

Are those women really breathing underwater?

Newton Perry knew how to make a splash in the aquatic entertainment world, having grown up nearly as much in the water as on land in Tampa and Ocala. A star swimmer and coach, he had served as the model for many of the images in the aquatic safety manuals produced by the American Red Cross in the 1920s, performed regularly in swimming exhibitions with his sisters, become a Hollywood consultant, and later trained Navy frogmen during World War II.

When Perry returned to civilian life, he immediately set about launching a novel business in Weeki Wachee, FL. He had devised a means of training young women to breathe underwater through oxygen hoses, and he quickly recruited his first class of "mermaids." On October 13, 1947, they gave their first performance, which included aquatic ballets, eating, drinking, and interacting with the fish in the spring, all underwater without needing to come to the surface for air.

ABC purchased and heavily promoted the park starting in 1959. They built a new underwater viewing area 16 feet below the surface with seating for 400, and still managed to sell out eight mermaid shows a day throughout the 1960s. The performances and costumes became more sophisticated, from reenacting Hans

The term weeki wachee is Seminole for "winding river" or "little spring," although "little" hardly does justice to the deepest known freshwater cave system in the United States.

The park has a riverboat cruise, kayak rentals, wildlife shows, and waterslides, but it's the mermaids that steal the show.

MAKING WAVES

What: Live Mermaid Shows at Weeki Wachee Springs State Park

Where: 6131 Commercial Way, Spring Hill

Cost: Adults, $13; children ages 6–12, $8; children ages 5 and under, free

Pro Tip: Leave your "land seals" at home—pets are not permitted in the park.

Christian Andersen's classic tale *The Little Mermaid* to staging elaborate picnics and doing synchronized underwater acrobatics.

High-profile visitors to park over the years have included Elvis Presley, Esther Williams, Kevin Smith, and Larry the Cable Guy. The Weeki Wachee mermaids have been featured in numerous films and TV series, as well as the music video for Kelly Clarkson's hit "Stronger."

Today the Weeki Wachee Mermaid shows continue to lure a steady stream of visitors with three shows each day, 365 days a year.

ROUGHING IT

Where did the Rough Riders stay in Tampa while awaiting their deployment to Cuba?

Today, you might easily drive past the marker inside Vila Brothers Park that explains the historical significance of the spot. Back in 1898, however, it would have been virtually impossible not to notice the 1,250 volunteers camped there as part of the 1st United States Volunteer Cavalry regiment, better known as the "Rough Riders."

Led by Colonel Leonard Wood and subsequently by Lieutenant Colonel Theodore Roosevelt, the Rough Riders were one of three regiments raised to fight in the Spanish–American War, and the only one to see combat (in Cuba).

Composed of college athletes, cowboys, miners, lawmen, trappers, and other outdoorsmen, over 600 of these Rough Riders departed from Port Tampa on June 24, 1898, to fight as "dismounted cavalry" (aka infantry). The remainder of the volunteers were left in Tampa due to a critical shortage of transportation. Those troops who did land in Cuba would go on to sustain the highest casualty rate of any American unit during that war and achieve legendary status in the process. Roosevelt himself was belatedly awarded the Medal of Honor for bravery on the field of battle.

Vila Brothers Park isn't the only place the Rough Riders left their hoof prints in Tampa. Outside the original Columbia Restaurant in Ybor City at the corner of Seventh Avenue and 22nd Street, you'll

---

"Roosevelt's Rough Riders" derived their nickname from the popular traveling Western show Buffalo Bill's Wild West and Congress of Rough Riders of the World.

The Rough Riders passed through many spots in Tampa, but Vila Brothers Park marks the place where most of them camped.

ONWARD TO GLORY

What: Traces of the Rough Riders

Where: Multiple locations, including Vila Brothers Park, 700 N. Armenia Ave., Tampa

Cost: Free

Pro Tip: Mark your calendar for 2028—that's when the time capsule at the monument in Ybor will be reopened to commemorate the 50th anniversary of Tampa's Rough Riders organization.

find a historical marker indicating that "The Rough Riders Rode By Here" in 1898. Walk less than a dozen blocks from this marker and you'll find the Rough Riders Memorial Park & Time Capsule. The Plant Museum has a more detailed display on the Rough Riders and the Spanish–American War, and at least a half dozen other markers and memorials dot the city.

VICTORY IS OURS

Is there a museum floating in Tampa Bay?

Of the 531 total Victory-class cargo ships produced in WWII for the Merchant Marine and US Navy, only three are in working condition today. Two of those are in California—the SS *Red Oak Victory* in Richmond and the SS *Lane Victory* in Los Angeles. The third, SS *American Victory*, has been docked in Tampa's Channelside district since 1996, when it was rescued from a fate as scrap metal.

The ship was completed on May 24, 1945, at the California Shipbuilding Corporation shipyard. From there, armed with eight 20mm-caliber Oerlikon guns, one three-inch 50 caliber gun, and one five-inch 38 caliber gun, it set sail and served in World War II, delivering cargo to Manila, Shanghai, Calcutta, and Port Said. Later, the ship would serve during the Korean and Vietnam Wars.

ACTA NON VERBA

What: American Victory Ship & Museum

Where: 705 Channelside Dr., Tampa

Cost: Members, free; adults, $10; seniors and students with ID, $8; veterans and children ages 4–12, $5. Special events have separate pricing.

Pro Tip: Tickets for the special events tend to sell out quickly, so if you plan to attend any of these, be sure to book them well in advance.

Near the entrance of the museum, see if you can spot a diagram of the German U-boat U-505, which was the first ship captured by Allied forces. Like the SS *American Victory*, today it is one of just a few of its type in existence. It is on display in Chicago.

Many of the restored rooms provide perspective into what "close quarters" mean aboard a ship.

In June of 1985 it underwent a $2.5 million restoration, but by this time its days as a military vessel were behind it.

Today, the ship has been reborn as the American Victory Ship & Museum, where visitors can view photos and historical information and explore the ship much as it would have appeared in the 1940s, complete with its steering stations, signaling equipment, massive three-level cargo holds, hospital, mess hall, weaponry, and cabins. There are educational and special events throughout the year, including Fourth of July fireworks and "Undead in the Water," which takes place weekends in October and transforms the ship into the site of a zombie outbreak.

STRAWBERRY FIELDS FOREVER

What are the official rules in a strawberry-stemming contest?

With more than 10,000 acres dedicated annually to producing the delicious dessert staple, Plant City takes its strawberries seriously. So much so that for 11 days each year you can experience every conceivable way to eat, compete, and interact with this prized product of central Florida.

For starters, there's plenty of food, from the obvious fresh strawberries, chocolate dipped strawberries, and strawberry shortcake to the less common strawberry Dole whip, crepes, and fritters, to the downright decadent strawberry sandwich from Carousel Hamburgers, which consists of a fried patty topped with strawberry mayonnaise and strawberry relish, served between two strawberry donuts.

After you've washed that all down with a strawberry lemonade, you can ride on the spinning strawberries, shop for strawberry cookbooks, watch some of the strawberry-product eating competitions, pose for a picture with mascots Mr. and Mrs. Berry, or bend the knee at the coronation of the annual Strawberry Queen.

And, of course, there are plenty of non-strawberry-related activities, including arts and crafts exhibitions in the Neighborhood Village, carnival rides in the Belle City Midway, youth livestock

---

Strawberries may be the headliner in Plant City, but kumquats, blueberries, and oranges all get their own festivals throughout the Tampa Bay area.

The fairgrounds feature a variety of strawberry-focused foods and amusements.

shows, merchandise vendors, and A-list musical performances that have included Reba McEntire, Aerosmith front man Steven Tyler, Willie Nelson, Rascal Flatts, 3 Doors Down, Alabama, and others. Sure, it may not be as big as Gasparilla, but the Plant City Strawberry Festival still ranks as one of the 40 top fairs in America and has remained essentially unchanged since it was first organized by the Plant City Lions Club in 1930.

THE HAND OF FATE

How dangerous is fishing along the Gulf Coast?

Fishing has always been an important part of life along the Gulf Coast, but it is not without its perils. Every year, fishermen go missing, both seasoned sailors and novices. The Florida Fishermen Lost at Sea Memorial (aka the Hand of Fate) is a powerful tribute to these unfortunate souls, made all the more striking for its incongruence with the surrounding tiki bars, surf shops, and tourist traps along the John's Pass boardwalk in Madeira Beach.

Unveiled on October 29, 2011, the nine-foot-tall sculpture was the result of a joint effort between the John's Pass Village and Boardwalk Merchant's Association, the Outdoor Arts Foundation, and artist Robert Bruce Epstein. Epstein's sculpture depicts an oxidized, sea green hand (perhaps belonging to Poseidon) from which rises a massive wave looming over a hapless fishing boat.

Inscribed around the base are the names of some of those commercial and recreational fishermen who never made it back home. While the exact number is unknown, the *St. Petersburg Times* estimated that more than 140 individuals have been lost in the Gulf of Mexico in Florida since 1933.

A poem inscribed on the front on the monument reads as follows:

I pray that I may live to fish . . .
until my dying day.
And when it comes to my last cast,
I then most humbly pray:
When in the Lord's great landing net
and peacefully asleep
That in His mercy I be judged
big enough to keep.

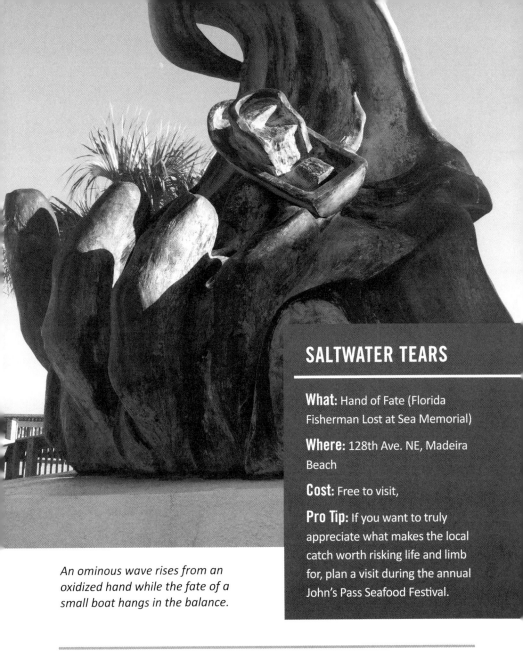

SALTWATER TEARS

What: Hand of Fate (Florida Fisherman Lost at Sea Memorial)

Where: 128th Ave. NE, Madeira Beach

Cost: Free to visit,

Pro Tip: If you want to truly appreciate what makes the local catch worth risking life and limb for, plan a visit during the annual John's Pass Seafood Festival.

An ominous wave rises from an oxidized hand while the fate of a small boat hangs in the balance.

The Hand of Fate isn't the only food-related monument in Madeira Beach—you can also find what is purported to be the world's largest chicken wing (replica) on the deck outside the Hooters restaurant there.

BRANCHING OUT

Does Clearwater have a slice of Dionysian paradise hiding in plain sight?

According to Hindu mythology, the kapok tree lures the souls of the damned with its red flowers and then torments them with its thorns and inedible fruit. We can safely assume that this wasn't the intention when Robert Hoyt planted a seedling kapok tree from India in front of his house in the 1870s, but the wonder that sprouted forth could certainly lend credence to the tree's allegedly mystical nature.

Among those visitors captivated by the tree over the years was one Richard B. Baumgardner, a musician and restaurateur who decided to acquire the land. Initially he envisioned building a performance venue but decided instead to create a one-of-a-kind restaurant. He began construction around 1948, and over the course of a decade he filled the garden and structure with columns and statuary imported from his travels throughout Europe. Piece by piece, the Kapok Tree Inn took form.

The restaurant was a huge success, achieving national and international acclaim. Even after Baumgardner's death in 1976, his family continued to operate the business, which ranked number 15 in the *Chicago Sun Times*' 1988 list of the best restaurants in the country. But at the height of its fame, on May 14, 1991, the restaurant suddenly closed.

Baumgardner's dream of creating a music venue was realized posthumously in 1977, when the Kapok Tree Corporation donated 38 acres to the City of Clearwater, upon which now sits Ruth Eckerd Hall, one of the area's premier concert halls.

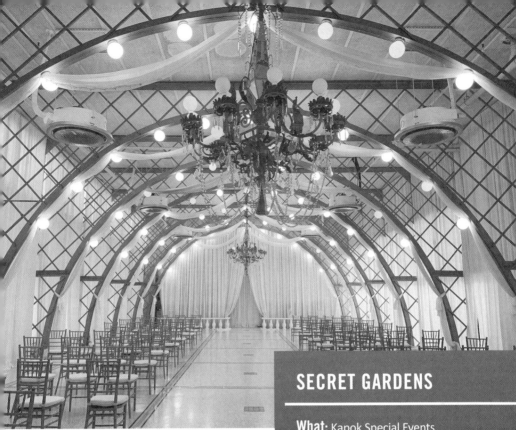

The garden and rooms continue to provide a magical setting for upscale events and weddings.

SECRET GARDENS

What: Kapok Special Events Center & Gardens

Where: 923 N. McMullen Booth Rd., Clearwater

Cost: The gardens are free.

Pro Tip: The gardens are open to the public from 9 a.m. to 5 p.m. Tuesday through Saturday.

The property changed hands and reopened in 1993 as a special event venue, with part of the facility leased out to the music company Sam Ash. Today it's a popular space for weddings and other special occasions, with lavish rooms featuring an inverted gold pyramid ceiling, hundreds of decorative, handmade glass grapes, palatial chandeliers, and a *Titanic*-styled main stairway. The gardens, with their beautifully overgrown stone walls, waterfalls, pond, and rows upon rows of statues and gargoyles, are open to the public.

SOUTH BY SOUTHWEST

What is St. Petersburg's connection to Western artwork?

The palm trees and waterfront of St. Petersburg don't exactly call to mind the pioneers of the Old West frontier, so after failing to find a building to house their vast private collection of Western artwork, Mary and Tom James (of Raymond James) decided to build their own . . . in the form of a sandstone canyon. The theme continues throughout the museum, with a waterfall cascading down the first-floor wall opposite the entranceway and the use of distinctly Western colors (like burnt sienna, rust, and sand) to serve as a visual guide through the different galleries.

Completed in April of 2018, the James Museum is one of the newest additions to the city's burgeoning cultural landscape. Inside it are about 400 works of art, ranging from sculptures and bronze castings to jewelry, and Native American art.

The couple has made the conscious decision to focus on supporting living artists. This means that while visitors will find some of what they would expect in the way of Western artwork like Native American beadwork, wildlife paintings, and big names like Remington and Russell, they'll also find abstract and pop works by artists such as Earl Biss and others.

In the center of the museum is the room known as the Jewel Box, which houses many of the collection's more literal gems. Designed and lit to resemble stepping into a gigantic purple

---

Just a couple highlights of the collection include *High Desert Clouds* by Ed Mell, and *Oh, You Wanted to See My Guns?* by Billy Schenck.

John Coleman's 1876 sculpture Gall—Sitting Bull—Crazy Horse.

geode, the Jewel Box is where you'll find an assortment of Native American jewelry.

Perhaps most interesting is the collection's window into the seldom-seen side of Western artwork, from paintings of the Chinese immigrants who helped build many of the railroads to unflinching and thought-provoking perspectives on the historically contentious relationship between the US government and Native Americans.

BUTTE-FUL

What: James Museum of Western & Wildlife Art

Where: 150 Central Ave., St. Petersburg

Cost: Adults, $20; students, military, and seniors, $15; youth ages 7–18, $10; children ages 6 and under, free

Pro Tip: Bring an extra layer—because artwork is best conserved at lower temperatures, the museum can get a little chilly.

ALMOST FAMOUS

How did New Port Richey nearly become the next Hollywood?

The name Thomas Meighan might not mean much to you today, but back in the 1920s he was a big deal. Think of him as the Bradley Cooper of silent films. Meighan decided to join the Florida real estate boom, purchasing land initially in Ocala and two years later in New Port Richey, where he built his home. Around the same time, golf champion Gene Sarazen also decided to build a home there (where he would invent the sand wedge).

Having both a big-name actor and a sports superstar living in town tied in nicely with the aspirations of the town's founders, who saw an opportunity to draw more celebrities and affluence to the area. Meighan and Sarazen were recruited to help promote New Port Richey among their circle of family and friends, and the results, initially, were quite successful. Actress Gloria Swanson acquired property there through a syndicate, and other visitors to the town included Leon Errol, Charlotte Greenwood, Blanche Ring, sportswriter Grantland Rice, writer Ring Lardner, and politician William Jennings Bryan.

The lobby of the Hacienda Hotel became a who's who of famous A-listers. The Meighan Theatre opened in 1926 with a screening, appropriately, of Meighan's film *The New Klondike*.

Just as things were looking up for New Port Richey, a confluence of factors would keep it from becoming New Hollywood. The humidity made the area a poor choice for movie production;

New Port Richey has had other famous residents since the Roaring Twenties—foremost among them, Johnny Cash.

New Port Richey's star-studded past is preserved and displayed at the Rao Musunuru, MD, Museum and Library.

Sarazen moved away after suing the developer of Jasmin Point and its golf club for his full wages; and last but not least, the 1929 stock market crash ushered in the Great Depression and indefinitely postponed New Port Richey's glamorous dreams.

Today the Meighan Theatre is known as the Richey Suncoast Theatre, and you can find vestiges of New Port Richey's star-studded past in the murals around town and in the Rao Musunuru, MD, Museum and Library.

HOLLYWOOD OF THE EAST

What: Traces of old Hollywood in New Port Richey

Where: Multiple locations, including the Richey Suncoast Theatre and the Rao Musunuru, MD, Museum and Library

Cost: Museum admission, $3

Pro Tip: You can leave your car at either the Gloria Swanson or Thomas Meighan Parking Areas.

A SUNNY PLACE FOR SHADY PEOPLE

What is bolita and how did it open the door to organized crime in Tampa?

When Vicente Martinez-Ybor established his city, it was a world unto itself, largely isolated from the rest of Tampa. The self-reliance that made Ybor City so culturally distinct also made it fertile ground for organized crime. As early as 1906, there were references to a sinister "Black Hand Society," the forerunner to today's Mafia.

Tampa might have gone unnoticed if not for one thing: bolita. This lottery game was massively popular in and beyond Ybor City, eventually generating as much as a billion dollars annually. It was also easy to rig, which made it even more attractive to the underworld. In 1919 the Volstead Act doused the already smoldering Cigar City Mafia with gallons of bootlegged Cuban rum, transforming it into a blazing criminal enterprise.

The first crime lord to emerge was Charlie Wall. Unlike most of his white-collar relatives, who became doctors and politicians, Wall opted to run the city's gambling, prostitution, human-trafficking, and drug trade.

Enter Ignacio Antinori to rival Wall's control of Tampa's underworld. Their turf wars in the late 1920s ushered in the Era of Blood—a 10-year period that saw dozens of bold, high-profile, and often unsolved murders. While Wall and Antinori were battling

---

The Tampa Mafia Tour is based on the book *Cigar City Mafia* by local author Scott M. Deitche. It is considered by many to be the most comprehensive source on the subject.

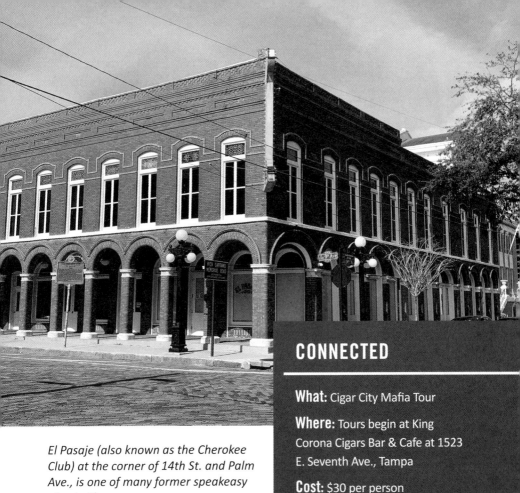

El Pasaje (also known as the Cherokee Club) at the corner of 14th St. and Palm Ave., is one of many former speakeasy sites in Ybor.

each other, Santo Trafficante Sr. stepped in and ruthlessly consolidated power. Trafficante and his son would reign for decades and serve as the mob's connection between Havana, Tampa, and Sicily—they were even approached by the CIA with a plot to assassinate Castro.

Sign on for the Tampa Mafia Tour if you want to see for yourself some of the more infamous former brothels, gambling dens, and street corners where many an unsavory character met with the business end of a sawed-off shotgun fired from a dark sedan.

THE MOTHER OF ALL SPECIALTY MUSEUMS

What does it feel like to wear a pregnancy vest and sit on a birthing chair?

In 2016 Joy Rose (former lead singer of Housewives on Prozac and Mamapalooza founder) relocated her collection of musical "mom"orabilia, art, and ephemera to a bungalow in the Artist Enclave of St. Peterburg's Historic Kenwood neighborhood, where it has been quietly gestating ever since. As the first and only exhibition and education center devoted to elucidating the science, history, and art of mothers, the Museum of Motherhood (MOM) is a unique addition to St. Pete's ever-evolving cultural scene.

The museum is divided into three primary sections: the science of motherhood, which

MAMARAMA

What: The Museum of Motherhood (MOM)

Where: 538 28th St. N., St. Petersburg

Cost: Visits with guided tours are free (donations are suggested and appreciated); special event pricing may vary.

Pro Tip: Future plans include "Tea & Tours" and "Wine & Wander" events, but for the time being you'll need to call or email INFO@MOMmuseum.org to schedule a visit.

After raising four children, Rose went back to graduate school to receive the first advanced degree in mother studies. Since then she has authored numerous academic papers and offers both courses and a residency program through the MOM.

The Museum of Motherhood offers a truly unique if seldom considered cultural perspective.

includes medical models, forceps, anatomically correct dolls, and pregnancy vests; a historical display featuring feminist pioneer Sojourner Truth and 1900s kitchen items; and a separate room filled with artwork. There's also a library and research area dedicated to this emerging field of study.

A clever display titled *Mother: The Job* presents photos of mothers performing the myriad unpaid activities associated with their role alongside paid professionals performing the same tasks, from accounting to food service, laundry, and transportation.

Activism is central to both the layout and concept of the museum, with a keen focus on those who care for and consciously raise the next generation of humans (and animals). Rose describes it as "a romp through the birth canal, herstory, and contemporary maternal art . . . peppered with feminist perspectives and bold commentary on the state of womanhood in America today. It's intended to enlighten, educate, and empower visitors, regardless of gender."

This message is also reflected in a large mirror, across which is written a quote by *Mother: The Job* artist Alexia Nye Jackson, reminding us that "One thing is for sure . . . there will never come a time when we no longer need to raise intelligent, motivated human beings to fill the workplace and this earth."

A CUT ABOVE THE REST

What makes a Tampa steakhouse legendary?

A rather plain-looking, windowless building that was once a strip mall in the South Howard (SoHo) District of Tampa belies the opulence and mouthwatering marvels within. Bern's Steak House opened in 1956, when Bern and Gert Laxer purchased the Beer Haven bar following the success of their small luncheonette, the Gator Juice Bar. To appease the landlord, who wasn't keen on alcohol sales, Bern and Gert operated it as a full-service restaurant. Over time their success allowed them to purchase the adjoining shops, for a total of eight dining rooms and seating for up to 350. They further expanded to include a wine cellar and offsite warehouse, the Harry Waugh Dessert Room (completed in 1985), and a sister restaurant, Haven (formerly SideBern's), which opened in 1996. Today David Laxer oversees the business his parents started.

The story is impressive, and the food has won a great many awards, but neither of these is what Bern's is really known for. To see what puts it in a class by itself, after dinner take the tour through the kitchen and down into the temperature-controlled wine cellar. With more than 100,000 bottles stored there (and another 600,000 or so in a warehouse), Bern's boasts the largest wine list of any restaurant in the world, and likely the largest private collection (exact rankings are difficult to gauge given the amount of wine they serve and replenish each day). Suffice it to say, it will be

---

From time to time, rare finds turn up in Bern's wine collection, like a $30,000 1947 double magnum of Château Latour.

The bland façade of this Tampa Bay institution stands in stark contrast to the lavish interior, exquisite food, and unrivaled wine selection.

HIGH STEAKS

What: Bern's Steak House

Where: 1208 S. Howard Ave., Tampa

Cost: Zagat's rates it $$$.

Pro Tip: The dress code for the dining room is business casual to semiformal, but there is a less formal lounge area as well.

more than enough to dazzle your sommelier friends.

Then it's up to the Harry Waugh Dessert Room, where decadent delights are served within semiprivate booths fashioned from redwood wine casks. The dessert room is so popular that plenty of visitors skip dinner entirely and head straight there, as seating is on a first-come, first-served basis.

A DEEP DIVE INTO TARPON SPRINGS

Were the Greeks the first sponge divers in Tarpon Springs?

You can't really describe Tarpon Springs without mentioning the sponge docks, and you can't discuss the sponge docks without first explaining Spongeorama, a store/museum that claims to offer the world's largest selection of natural sponges. Looking to dive deeper? Just watch the wonderfully vintage informational video that plays on a loop in the small visitor section. You'll learn how, in 1905, John Michael Cocoris collaborated with John Cheney to recruit Greek sponge divers from the Dodecanese Islands and transform the local sponge business into a multimillion-dollar industry. As of this writing, the museum section of Spongeorama is closed due to hurricane damage, but the gift shop is sure to reveal everything

A VENTURE THAT HOLDS WATER

What: Spongeorama and the Tarpon Springs Sponge Docks

Where: 510 Dodecanese Blvd., Tarpon Springs

Cost: Free to visit

Pro Tip: There's a lot more worth exploring in Tarpon Springs, including the Leepa-Rattner Museum of Art, the Replay Museum of vintage arcade and pinball games, and a number of stellar craft breweries.

A visit to Rose Hill Cemetery will reveal that some of the area's earliest sponge divers were actually from the Bahamas and the Florida Keys.

Spongeorama is just one of the many unusual things to see in Tarpon Springs.

sponge-related that you never knew you never needed but always wanted.

From Spongeorama you can catch a tour boat or walk further along the docks. You might find some treasures in the souvenir shops, but the real catch is the cuisine. You won't find better, more authentic moussaka, souvlaki, or spanakopita anywhere in Tampa Bay, maybe even in all of Florida.

And if you really want to soak up the local culture, head to St. Nicholas Church early on January sixth each year to celebrate the largest Epiphany (Theophany) in America. Around noon you can follow a procession of young sponge divers from the church to Tarpon Springs Bayou for the casting of the cross—known colloquially as "the toss for the cross." The boys take their positions on rafts and canoes and wait for an archbishop to cast the cross into the waters. The first boy to retrieve it receives a year's worth of blessings for his family's boats and has his name inscribed on the monument in front of the church.

THE GREATEST SHOW ON EARTH

What became of John and Mable Ringling's fortune?

The name Ringling probably calls to mind elephants performing tricks, trapeze artists, clowns, cotton candy, human cannonballs, and all things circus related. But the cultural impact that John and Mable Ringling left on their adopted home requires every inch of a 66-acre museum complex to capture.

To start with, there's Ca' d'Zan ("House of John"), the Venetian Gothic mansion overlooking the bay where the couple wintered. Finished in 1926 with 56 rooms and a price tag of $1.5 million, the home has been restored to its original glory and included in the American Institute of Architects' Florida Chapter list *Florida Architecture: 100 Years. 100 Places.*

Prolific art collectors, the Ringlings amassed a veritable treasure trove of paintings by old masters like Velázquez, Rubens, El Greco, and others. Their collection today fills the 21-gallery art museum and courtyard, which wouldn't be a complete Renaissance garden without a replica of Michelangelo's David from the Chiurazzi Foundry in Italy.

The main attraction for most visitors, however, is the Circus Museum, which features old posters, costumes, interactive displays, and the Ringlings' private railcar. It also contains the world's largest miniature circus. A mindboggling achievement, it comprises 42,000

Once one of the wealthiest men in America (valued at over $200 million), John Ringling was left deeply in debt by the Great Depression, and at the time of his death in 1936, he was all but penniless.

The mural in the Tibbals Learning Center highlights many of the most famous Ringling Brothers and Barnum & Bailey performers, including Lancelot the unicorn.

individual pieces, each of which was painstakingly handmade by Howard Tibbals over the course of 60 years.

The Bayfront Gardens, the Tibbals Learning Center, and the Historic Asolo Theater round out the museum complex.

After 146 years, the Ringling Bros. and Barnum & Bailey Circus may have held its final performance in 2017, but you can still bask in the afterglow of the greatest show on earth anytime you like at The Ringling.

UNDER THE BIG TOP

What: The Ringling

Where: 5401 Bay Shore Rd., Sarasota

Cost: General admission is adults, $25; seniors, $23; children ages 6–17, $5; members and children ages 5 and under, free. The general admission does not include entry to Ca' d'Zan.

Pro Tip: Don't try this at home: taming lions and being launched from cannons are things best left to the pros.

ON THE ROCKS

Aren't there laws against opening up a bar in your house?

To call Mahuffer's a hole in the wall would imply that it actually has walls. It's really more of a shack that at first glance appears to be held together entirely by the dollar bills and undergarments tacked to the ceiling. But the bar, like the man who operated it for over 30 years, is indeed legendary.

Separating fact from fiction regarding John "Mahuffer" Susor is made more complicated by his death in 2008, which elevated his status from bookie and local miscreant to full-blown antihero. The pistol-packing proprietor, who was married nine times, decided at one point to open a bait shop in his home. Since the fishermen would linger there to drink, he started charging them, and thus, around 1971, Mahuffer's was born.

Operating without a license was enough to incur the ire of local law enforcement, but John took things to the next level, and countless altercations occurred. He became a regular at the local courthouse on charges ranging from assault and battery to vandalism to illegal gambling. Regardless, Mahuffer's survived long enough to become an institution.

Today, Mahuffer's is owned and operated by his daughter, who decided at long last to bring the bar up to code, using the money from the bar ceiling. Despite the change in ownership,

---

Most folks either love or loathe Mahuffer's—the sign out front calls it the "Wurst bar on the Beech," but that hasn't kept it from winning multiple awards, including "Best of Tampa Bay."

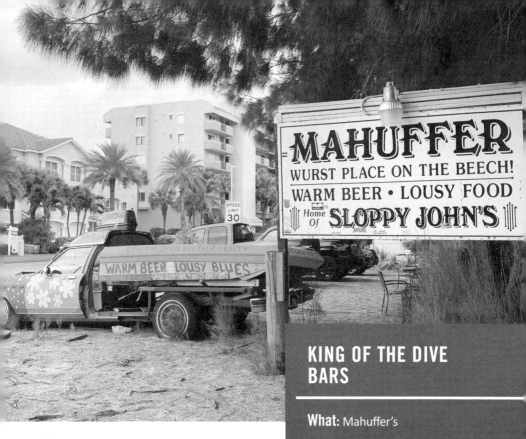

Locals consider Mahuffer's an eyesore, an institution, or both.

it has maintained a distinctly outsider appeal—every inch of usable space has been scribbled on and carved with obscenities. Some of the chairs look like they've been lifted from a local schoolhouse. There's the prow of a boat rumored to have belonged to Marilyn Monroe. There's an iguana cage. And there are stories galore that longtime regulars will happily share with you for the cost of a drink.

KING OF THE DIVE BARS

What: Mahuffer's

Where: 19201 Gulf Blvd., Indian Shores

Cost: The cheapest beer and mixed drinks you're likely to find in the Tampa Bay area

Pro Tip: Even though it's technically "up to code," you might still want to make sure you're up to date on all your shots.

TRIASSIC PARK

What are all those life-sized dinosaur sculptures doing by the highway in Plant City?

Author Michael Crichton wasn't the only one in the 1990s who thought the idea of a dinosaur-themed outdoor park sounded pretty compelling. Swedish businessman Christer Svensson was well versed in creating dinosaurs in Australia and Japan prior to relocating to Florida and purchasing what had previously been a gator farm in Plant City.

Thus was born Dinosaur World, the first in what has grown to be a chain of three parks under the same name (the other two being in Cave City, KY, and Glen Rose, TX). Its claim to being "The World's Largest Dinosaur Park" is tough to argue with, as there are over 150 life-sized dinosaur statues throughout the park, constructed from fiberglass, steel, and concrete. These fixtures are posed in various daily dinosaur activities, more or less as they would have appeared when they roamed the earth.

The park's astonishingly large assortment of dinosaurs includes not only the "classics" like the stegosaurus, brontosaurus, and Tyrannosaurus rex, but also a number of lesser-known dinosaurs like the pachycephalosaur—the largest of the head-butting dinosaurs, according to the information plaque—and the avimimus, which has a distinctly chicken-like appearance.

In the land of the mouse god (aka Disney), it's survival of the fittest among the countless theme parks and attractions. After more than 20 years, though, Dinosaur World has proved both its staying power and its ability to evolve.

Dinosaur World features interactive shows, a small fossil museum, and more than 150 life-like dinosaur sculptures.

In addition to the boardwalk that winds past outdoor displays, the park includes a fossil dig sand pit for kids, picnic and dino-themed playground areas, a small museum (which includes a couple of obligatory animatronics), multiple interactive shows and exhibits, and a 7,000-square-foot gift shop. The entire park is also dog friendly.

NO BONES ABOUT IT

What: Dinosaur World

Where: 5145 Harvey Tew Rd., Plant City

Cost: Standard admission for adults, $16.95; seniors, $14.95; children ages 3–12, $11.95; children ages 2 and under, free. Excavation passes are extra.

Pro Tip: There are plenty of spots to dine with the dinos, but you'll need to pack your own meal. Food is not served within the park.

AGAINST THE GRAIN

How did Treasure Island earn the title of Sand Sculpture Capital of Florida?

It's hard to compete with local celebrations that include a global mural festival and a weeklong pirate party, but the beach town of Treasure Island was more than up to the challenge, giving rise to one of the Tampa Bay area's most unique annual competitions. Sanding Ovations takes place in late November each year and brings, by invitation, a dozen master sculptors from all over the world to compete in conjuring astoundingly lifelike, sophisticated, and otherworldly artworks from the most abundant and readily accessible local material. With more than $12,000 in prizes at stake, you can bet that the artists dig deep to bring forth truly over-the-top, three-dimensional masterpieces.

The five-day event begins with an artist meet and greet and then launches into a beach festival complete with food and music. You'll find a variety of creative vendors offering hand-carved

THE FINE ART OF BEACHCOMBING

What: Sanding Ovations

Where: Treasure Island Beach at 104th Ave. & Gulf Blvd.

Cost: Free

Pro Tip: Treasure Island is a small beach town, which means that hotels and public parking fill up quickly. Plan ahead and be prepared for crowds.

Treasure Island got its name when a local hotel owner planted and then "discovered" several wooden treasure chests on his property as a promotional gimmick.

The relationship between human beings and the environment is a frequent theme at Sanding Ovations.

wooden tiki masks, customized metalworks, and ornate crowns constructed out of seashells. Of course, you can always just pull up a folding chair or blanket and watch the internationally renowned sand sculptors at work, patiently applying their talent and tools to pack, shave, and texture sand, giving form to their visions. Judging takes place on the fourth day, followed by an awards ceremony and fireworks display.

From year to year and artwork to artwork, you'll find some common themes, such as mankind's impact on the environment, sustainability, and other social and ecological topics.

PROTECT AND SERVE

How have Tampa's police uniforms, vehicles, and equipment changed over the years?

Even before you enter the small museum attached to the ground floor of the Tampa Police Department headquarters, you might be struck by the memorial out front honoring those who made the ultimate sacrifice while keeping the city and its citizens safe.

Once inside, visitors can see a collection that spans over a century of history—Tampa's police force dates back to 1886. Just a few of the harder-to-miss items include one of the city's first police helicopters, early police motorcycles, a 1924 Model T squad car, an old police callbox, a bomb disposal robot, uniforms, badges, and an arsenal of weapons confiscated from criminals.

There is an extensive rogue's gallery featuring original mug shots and fingerprint cards of infamous criminals like John Dillinger and Bonnie and Clyde. There is also a powerful memorial section with a wall featuring all of Tampa's officers killed in the line of duty. In this section of the museum you also find the tombstone of John McCormick, who, on September 26, 1895, became the first of Tampa's officers to lose his life while on duty. Members of the Tampa Police Department remembered here for their service extend beyond humans and include Queenie, who was Tampa's first police dog.

If you're interested in the history of Tampa's emergency responders, you can also stop in at the Tampa Firefighters Museum, which features a number of interesting artifacts and a powerful 9/11 memorial.

The Tampa Police Museum features uniforms, badges, weaponry, vehicles, and other tools of the law enforcement trade.

The museum officially opened in 1998—prior to this, for roughly four decades, it had been one officer's private collection. It has been considerably augmented since then with various artifacts and a small gift shop. The most valuable and unique asset in the museum, however, is unquestionably the collective knowledge and experience of its volunteer staff, who can share a wealth of memories and personal accounts.

THAT'S HOW WE ROLL

What goes into making a perfect cigar?

At its peak, with 252 individual cigar makers, Ybor City once produced as many as 700 million cigars annually. Of course, that was before the Great Depression, before cigarettes became popular and brought with them machine rolling technologies, before President John F. Kennedy placed an embargo on Cuban cigars, before the FDA's anti-tobacco campaign, and long before vaping became a thing.

But despite all these challenges, cigar making in Ybor hasn't been snuffed out. Yanko Maceda, founder of Tabanero Cigars, is one of several boutique manufacturers preserving the industry that earned Tampa the name Cigar City. Founded in 2007, Tabanero now employs four full-time artisans who produce 12,000 hand-rolled cigars each month. Its operations have expanded to encompass end-to-end capabilities, with its own on-site humidor, laser cutters, and box-making equipment, not to mention an exclusive deal that makes it the sole provider of Naviera coffee in the state of Florida.

Tabanero offers courses ranging from 101 for novices to more advanced education for seasoned cigar aficionados. The company also offers a tour of its operation, covering the history of cigar making in Ybor, as well as a first-hand look at each step

---

Be sure to talk to Steven, who gives both cigar factory and Ybor City ghost tours. Few folks are friendlier or more knowledgeable about the myriad secrets of Ybor City that make it uniquely weird and wonderful.

Tabanero is keeping Ybor's culture and signature industry alive.

in the process. You'll see how the tobacco is grown, cured, rolled, stored, packaged, and distributed, while sipping a small complimentary cup of café con leche. And you'll pick up some tips along the way, such as the ideal temperature and humidity for storing and aging your cigars and why a thin dusting of white powder means that your cigars have been aged to perfection.

HECHO A MANO

What: Tabanero Cigar Factory Tour

Where: 1601 E. 7th Ave., Tampa

Cost: Tours are $15.

Pro Tip: If you have respiratory difficulties or an aversion to spending 90 minutes in a dense cloud of cigar smoke, this might not be the best tour for you.

BEACHFRONT SURREAL ESTATE

Who has the most famous mustache in St. Petersburg?

The name Salvador Dalí is synonymous with surrealism—dreamlike and impossible landscapes populated by melting clocks, animals roaming about on elongated, stilt-like legs, and a bevy of optical illusions. Outside of his hometown in Figueres, Spain, the largest collection of Dalí's work is in downtown St. Petersburg.

The collection belonging to Reynolds and Eleanor Morse, which includes over 2,000 pieces, first came to St. Pete in 1982. In 2011 the original location was replaced with the museum, which has an unmistakably surreal design, with a freeform geodesic glass bubble expanding from the first floor and stairways that spiral upward, tapering off into nothing—a structure that surely Dalí himself would have approved of.

Featured prominently on just about any travel website or brochure, the museum may not qualify as obscure these days, but it is certainly weird and wonderful. Within you'll find many of Dalí's famous works, including *The Hallucinogenic Toreador*, *Geopoliticus Child Watching the Birth of the New Man*, *The Discovery of America by Christopher Columbus*, and *Portrait of My Dead Brother*.

As a world-class museum, visitors will find rotating exhibits that highlight Dalí's connection to other artists, such as Frida Kahlo, René

The museum building was designed by Yann Weymouth of the design firm HOK, and that glass bubble on the first floor is called "the Enigma." It reaches a height of 75 feet and is composed of 1,062 triangular pieces of glass.

70

In addition to paintings, you'll find photography and sculptures like Lobster Telephone *at the Dalí.*

Magritte, M. C. Escher, Pablo Picasso, and a great many others. And if a stroll through the exhibits doesn't augment your reality enough, the museum has recently released an augmented reality app for your smartphone, giving visitors a new way to experience Dalí's vision and craft.

HELLO, DALÍ

What: The Dalí (Salvador Dalí Museum)

Where: 1 Dalí Blvd., St. Petersburg

Cost: General admission for adults ages 18 to 65, $25; discounts for seniors, military and police, firefighters, educators, students, and children. Admission is free for children ages 5 and under. Discounts after 5 p.m. on Thursdays.

Pro Tip: Hang on to your wristband after your visit and tie it to the tree behind the museum, which has become a collaborative, living artwork of its own.

BLOOD AND GOLD

Where did exploration of the North American continent by Europeans begin?

Of all the visitors throughout Florida's history, Pánfilo de Narváez surely ranks among the absolute worst. Known for both his cruelty and his insatiable lust for gold, Narváez set sail from Spain with 600 men on June 17, 1527. By the time he landed near St. Petersburg on April 15, 1528, his crew had dwindled to 300, with 140 deserting him in Santo Domingo and, presumably, the rest being lost in a hurricane near Cuba.

Undeterred, Narváez promptly set about torturing and butchering the local Tocobaga tribespeople he encountered, convinced that they were withholding treasure from him. Having previously failed to thwart Cortés in Mexico, where he lost an eye, he didn't plan to come away empty-handed from this expedition.

As he marched his men north in search of nonexistent riches, the casualties mounted. Those Spaniards who weren't killed by the natives succumbed to storms, starvation, and sickness. After eight years, just four survivors made their way on foot all the way to Northern Mexico.

Following Narváez's disastrous expedition, Juan Ortiz was sent from Spain to investigate and see if any of the party had survived.

There's a legend about the origin of Spanish moss in Florida, in which a bird flies off with a piece of gold and a conquistador goes chasing after it. The conquistador becomes lodged in the tree and dies, but his beard continues to grow and becomes the grey moss that hangs from tree branches.

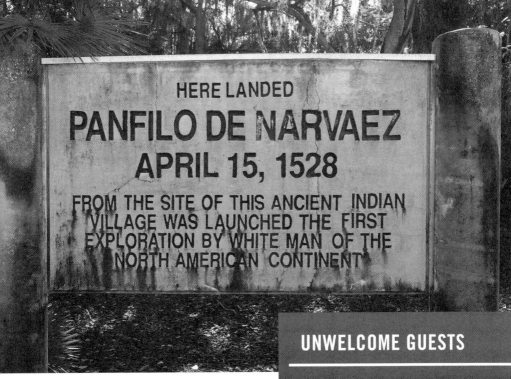

HERE LANDED

PANFILO DE NARVAEZ
APRIL 15, 1528

FROM THE SITE OF THIS ANCIENT INDIAN VILLAGE WAS LAUNCHED THE FIRST EXPLORATION BY WHITE MAN OF THE NORTH AMERICAN CONTINENT

Panfilo de Narvaez is remembered not for finding unimaginable riches but, rather, for inflicting unimaginable cruelty.

Legend has it that Ortiz ran afoul of the locals, who weren't particularly happy with the previous Spanish visitors and took him prisoner. His execution was stayed, however, by the chief's daughter, Ulele, who convinced her father to take Ortiz as a slave instead of roasting him alive. This story would be recorded when de Soto found Ortiz living among the natives—and likely became the basis of the Pocahontas story.

As for Narváez, his final resting place is unknown, but you can find the site of his landing, known as the Jungle Prada Site, populated today by peacocks rather than bloodthirsty conquistadores.

PIRATES, POLITICIANS, AND PIONEER PRIESTS

What can you expect to find at Tampa's oldest public burial ground?

Oaklawn Cemetery opened in 1850 as a place for "White and Slave, Rich and Poor." Among its estimated 1,700 graves you'll find many members of Tampa's founding families. They keep company with the soldiers of seven different wars, a Florida governor, Tampa's first harbor captain, two Florida Supreme Court justices, framers of all five Florida constitutions, and 13 mayors of Tampa, including the city's first, Judge Joseph Bradford Lancaster. Not to mention a couple of Cuban pirates like Mr. Hubbard and José "El Indio" Perfino.

Saint Louis Catholic Cemetery, established in 1874, occupies the northwest section of Oaklawn. Notable graves and markers in this section include cigar boss Vicente Martinez-Ybor, five pioneer priests, and Cecilia Morse, who started

ETCHED IN STONE

What: Oaklawn Cemetery

Where: 606 E. Harrison St., Tampa

Cost: Free

Pro Tip: A self-guided walking tour is available at https://www.tampagov.net/parks-and-recreation/parks-and-natural-areas/cemeteries/oaklawn-walking-tour.

Other unique facts and facets of Oaklawn: When the USS *Sagamore* bombarded Tampa on July 1, 1862, an eight-inch shell landed in the cemetery. There's also a hungry tree that is slowly devouring a tombstone near the Kennedy family plot.

Notable epitaphs include Elpenice Moore, who "died at sea," and Mr. Hubbard, "a Cuban pirate found dead in woods."

Tampa's Catholic parochial education. This section also features a monument to the many slaves buried in Oaklawn.

Oaklawn has two mass graves: one for the victims of yellow fever, and another for the 102 soldiers and settlers originally laid to rest at Fort Brooke. There are also 2,000-year-old Native American remains that were reinterred at Oaklawn after being discovered in 1987 during construction downtown.

The best-known grave in Oaklawn is probably that of William and Nancy Ashley. In public, William was a prominent white civic leader and Nancy was his black servant. Behind closed doors, they lived as man and wife in defiance of the laws and customs of the time. The inscription on their tombstone reads: "Master and Servant, faithful to each other in that relation in life, in death they are not separated. Stranger consider and be wiser, in the grave all human distinction of race or cast mingle together in one common dust."

UPCYCLED

Is that a Christmas tree in the center of a junkyard off by the side of I-75?

In 1958 a then eight-year-old Joe Brown learned a lesson that changed his life when an art teacher taught him to transform something that most would see as garbage—an empty Gerber baby bottle, in this case—into a work of art. The class was his introduction to ideas such as creative reuse and recycling. Another fact: his art teacher had left for Hiroshima from Hong Kong, something Joe Brown would never forget.

Of course, no one could have predicted that some 30 years later, after having made a career in the materials management industry, Brown would apply his childhood lessons in transformation and rebirth to his property in Tampa and even to himself, adopting the name by which he's far better known: Hong Kong Willie.

While green and sustainable living may seem like a relatively new concept to some, Brown has been doing it since the 1980s, when he built his cred as an outsider artist and sculptor. Subsequently, he acquired some land in Tampa and rapidly transformed it into a unique outsider art compound where driftwood, buoys, fishing nets, street signs, broken toys, car parts, glass shards, and even a rusted old helicopter can find new life as artwork.

Hong Kong Willie is located just a short drive from the Big Top Flea Market, another place where you can spend all day sifting treasure from trash.

The helicopter has been removed from the property, but you can still find plenty of other fascinating artworks.

SALVAGED

What: Hong Kong Willie

Where: 12212 Morris Bridge Rd., Tampa

Cost: A pound of red worms (that's about 450 individual worms) goes for $49.99. Artwork pricing varies.

Pro Tip: While most visitors flock to his larger, harder-to-miss pieces like the Buoy Tree, don't miss some of his lesser-known works like Miriosity, which showcases Brown's talent as an artist.

While the visual cacophony that Brown has assembled in, on, and around his property is a big draw for out-of-towners, it's the worms that bring most of the locals by—specifically, the Florida redworms, which Brown cultivates and sells primarily for composting (although plenty of customers swear by them as fishing bait).

Whether you're looking for bait worms or artwork, you're bound to find something worth a visit to the inimitable Hong Kong Willie.

CITY IN A SANDWICH

Where and how did the Cuban sandwich originate?

Every city has its iconic foods, and in Tampa that can only mean the Cuban sandwich (fried grouper being a close second). But where and how the Cuban sandwich came into existence is the subject of a long-standing food fight between Miami and Tampa.

The key components are the same in both cities: Cuban bread, ham, roasted pork, Swiss cheese, sliced dill pickles, and yellow mustard, together toasted in a plancha (essentially, a panini press without the grooves). They differ in that Tampa sandwich makers add Genoa salami (a tribute to the city's Italian immigrants), while Miami opts to include mayonnaise. In spite of these differences, both cities agree that the meal originated with the Cuban cigar factory workers who needed a simple and affordable lunch.

Most locals will tell you that the bread is really the magical component that separates a true Cuban sandwich from the average ham and cheese. Credit for this carbohydrate masterpiece often goes to Francisco Ferlita, a Sicilian baker in Ybor City who, somewhere around 1896, scoured the top of his bread with a palmetto leaf and squared the edges, designating it "Cuban bread." If the bread was invented in Ybor, it would certainly help validate Tampa's claim on the original.

The true ancestry of the Cuban sandwich probably dates to the Taíno tribe in Cuba, where it would have consisted of cassava bread stuffed with fish and bird meat—pork didn't show up on the island's menu until Europeans arrived.

If you're in the mood for another Tampa specialty, try an order of scachatta.

LONCHANDO

What: The Cuban Sandwich

Where: La Segunda Bakery, 2512 N. 15th St., Tampa

Cost: $8.99 for the Cuban

Pro Tip: Putting mayo on a Cuban sandwich is a lot like putting ketchup on a Chicago dog—it's just not something you need to do. Ever.

It's safe to say that for most folks, what matters far more than the sandwich's point of origin is its final destination, meaning their bellies. So, from what port, or sandwich shop rather, should you embark on this culinary adventure? There is an abundance of options, but virtually everyone ranks La Segunda at or near the top of the list, with La Teresita, Columbia, and Bodega all close contenders.

DOWN THE RABBIT HOLE

Have there been any Bigfoot sightings in the Tampa Bay area?

You'll smell it before you see it. At least, that's what local lore says about skunk apes, which you could think of as extremely pungent, swamp-dwelling cousins of the sasquatch. Despite numerous reports and sightings throughout Florida over the years, the skunk ape is considered a "cryptid"—a creature whose existence is unsubstantiated. Some speculate that these sightings were actually of black bears, while others, such as the National Park Service, consider it a hoax.

Escape rooms, on the other hand, are far easier to spot than skunk apes—it seems like there's one on just about every other block. But the clever folks at Rabbit Hole Escape Games have found a way to bring the two together, putting a uniquely Floridian twist on the popular group activity.

The business offers two different scenarios, each an hour in length, in which skunk apes

APE ESCAPE

What: Rabbit Hole Escape Games

Where: 5205 N. Florida Ave., Tampa

Cost: $29 per player

Pro Tip: Relax, have fun, and put your head together with your teammates. Even if you don't solve the mysteries, you'll still be let out after an hour.

If you want to examine "evidence" of skunk apes for yourself and you don't mind a long drive from Tampa, stop by the Skunk Ape Research Headquarters in Ochopee.

Rabbit Hole Escape Games has found an ingenious way to combine local skunk ape lore with puzzles and brain teasers.

play a leading role. The first, "Shadows of the Skunk Ape," puts players in the role of park rangers at Cabbage Lake State Park trying to recover an item stolen from the park while evacuating campers ahead of a storm. Of course, things are further complicated by the skunk ape. The second adventure, "Lore of the Skunk Ape," casts your team as cryptozoology students on your way to see your professor. Upon arriving, though, you find that a rival team has arrived first, made off with the professor's research, and locked you in an RV.

If following clues that involve Florida's most malodorous cryptid isn't your thing, you can always check out some of the other activities at Rabbit Hole Escape Games.

THE GULP COAST

What's the difference between growlers, howlers, and crowlers?

Throughout the country, craft breweries are having a prolonged moment, but Tampa Bay has taken the phenomenon to another level entirely. The Gulp Coast Craft Brewery Trail details 41 establishments from St Petersburg to Tarpon Springs, and another 42 between Tampa and Venice. The Tampa Bay Ale Trail lists 71 of them. Expand the radius farther to the east and you are easily looking at 100 breweries, each serving up its own unique concoctions.

Among the myriad options, you have perennial favorites like 3 Daughters, Overflow, Coppertail, and Angry Chair. But that still leaves plenty of room for the specialty brewpubs. If you want Oktoberfest all year long, you can stop into Lagerhaus for a beer and schnitzel. If small-batch ales are more your speed, then Southern Lights has something you'll like. In the mood for sours? Arkane Aleworks has you covered. Want to watch a cult classic horror movie while sipping a People Are Lestrange or an Evil Dead Smoked Red? Grindhaus Brew Lab is your answer.

Many of the local breweries pride themselves on being dog friendly (none more so than Pinellas Ale Works, or PAW, for short), so your four-legged drinking buddy can join you. You'll also find

---

Stop by the St. Pete Store & Visitors Center for a free Gulp Coast Passport to collect stamps for rewards. If you're really ambitious, you can also go online to tampabaybeerweek.com and order the larger Ale Trail Passport or the statewide Hop Passport.

Crooked Thumb is just one of the microbreweries with stellar outdoor seating.

DOWN THE HATCH

What: A staggeringly vast assortment of craft breweries

Where: All over Tampa Bay

Cost: The Gulp Coast Passport is free; the Ale Trail Passport costs $25 but includes BOGO offers on second visits to participating breweries. Both are printed in limited supply.

Pro Tip: Drink responsibly and never, ever get behind the wheel if you're buzzed.

plenty of live music, bar trivia nights, beer gardens, arcade games, and other activities to keep you entertained. And you may be happily surprised to discover that many of these brewpubs put as much care into their food as they do their beverages. Just try the grilled cheese waffle sandwich at 3 Keys and see if you don't agree.

GLASS WIZARDRY

Who is the most famous living glass artist?

Even if you're not familiar with the name Dale Chihuly, you've probably seen his work. A world-renowned pioneer in the studio glass movement, for more than five decades he's been bringing prismatic dreamscapes to life with his unique, organic, and large-scale glass artworks and installations. In 2017, through the Morean Arts Center in St. Petersburg, many of his creations found a new home in the first custom-designed building to showcase his work. This 11,000-square-foot collection includes multiple rooms and hallways featuring either individual works or sets, as well as a glass-ceiling hallway that creates an effect similar to wandering through the inside of a kaleidoscope.

On display are several massive chandeliers that look somewhat like a colony of crystalline giant tube worms decided to celebrate

COMMITTED TO TRANSPARENCY

What: The Chihuly Collection

Where: 720 Central Ave., St. Petersburg

Cost: Adults, $20; seniors and military, $18; students ages 6–18, $13; children ages 5 and under, free

Pro Tip: Hold on to your tickets—they're good for a free glassblowing demonstration across the street at the Morean Glass Studio & Hot Shop.

The title of this chapter pays tribute to another world-famous creative master: Stephen King, who became a resident of Sarasota in April 2001 (*Wizards and Glass* is the title of the fourth book in his Dark Tower series).

Chihuly's glass artworks call to mind colorful colonies of crystalline tubeworms.

Mardi Gras together. Other works featured include the icy, electric blue *Tumbleweeds* suspended in its own room, the Macchia Forest of organic bowls, and the bright, celebratory *Mille Fiori*, as well as various *Ikebana* and *Niijima Floats*.

Also on display are many of the artist's works on paper, as well as pieces from both his *Sea Form* and *Venetian* series. Interestingly, one of those *Venetians* on display was once stolen from the collection, only to be returned the following day in a crudely taped box. The work was unharmed, but it had also been wiped clean of any fingerprints and at the time of this writing, the case remains unsolved.

In the interest of transparency, the Chihuly Collection isn't the only place to find astounding glass artworks in town. The Imagine Museum includes major works from around the world, and there are a plethora of talented local artists like Susan Gott of Phoenix Glass Studio.

THE MOST CELEBRATED PIRATE WHO PROBABLY NEVER LIVED (PAGE 4)

FLORIDA'S FIRST MAGIC KINGDOM (PAGE 10)

SHINE ON (PAGE 16)

SOUTH BY SOUTHWEST (PAGE 46)

ROOFTOP ODDITIES (PAGE 18)

BRANCHING OUT (PAGE 44)

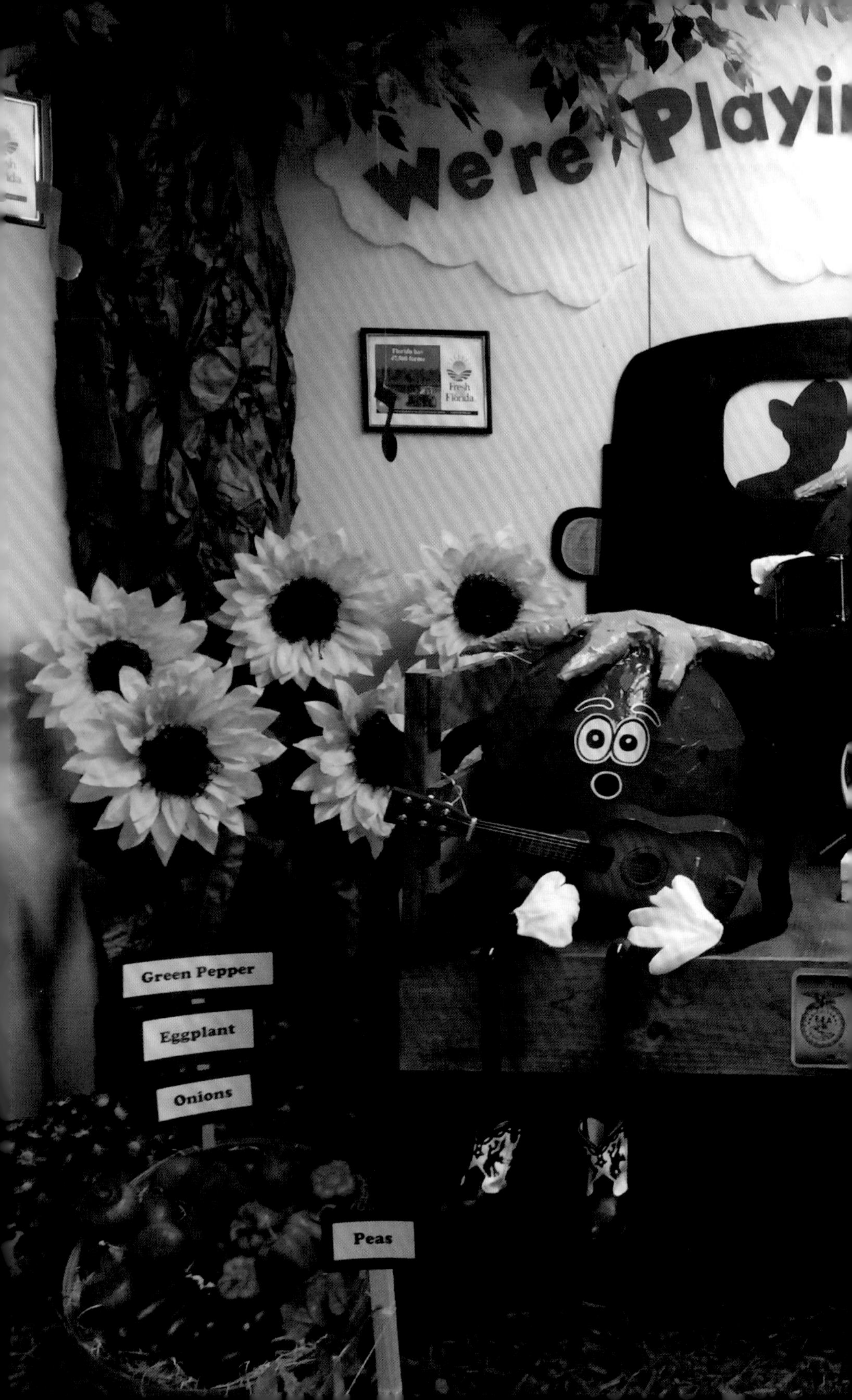
We're
Fresh Florida
Green Pepper
Eggplant
Onions
Peas

STRAWBERRY FIELDS FOREVER (PAGE 40)

GLASS WIZARDRY (PAGE 84)

FLOTSAM AND JETSAM (PAGE 146)

CRACKER COUNTRY (PAGE 14)

MORE THAN JUST A WHIM (PAGE 188)

THE WARLOCK OF WESLEY CHAPEL (PAGE 118)

CINEMA PARADISO

What's so special about the Tampa Theatre?

Walking through the ornate, gilded entranceway to the Tampa
Theatre is like passing through a portal to an alternate reality. The
entranceway opens up to a Mediterranean-styled courtyard and
ceiling painted to resemble a starry sky. Gargoyles, fleurs-de-lis,
Greek statues, and Spanish and Persian accents make the interior a
veritable jazz age dreamscape.

Built in 1926 by architect and movie palace pioneer John
Eberson, the Tampa Theatre was said to be one of his personal
favorites. It combines many of the architectural elements he
encountered during his trips throughout Florida and features an
original Wurlitzer Theatre Organ.

Over time, single-screen movie theatres became less popular
and patrons moved out from the city to the suburbs, which led to
the theatre's decline until the 1970s, when the city council enacted
a plan to rescue the theatre and turn it into a community film and
cultural center. In 1978 it was listed on the National Register of
Historic Places and today is considered a city landmark.

It's such a beloved venue, in fact, that a number of former
patrons and employees are said to still visit . . . from beyond the
grave. The best known of these is Fink Finley, who leaves a faint
scent of lilac and cigarette smoke along his path from the balcony

---

The Tampa Theatre has over 600 events a year, from
films to educational programs, corporate events, and
backstage tours. During October, you can also take a
ghost tour, where you'll learn more about Fink Finley
and the theater's other permanent residents.

Today the Tampa Theatre has been revitalized and restored to its 1920s glory.

CENTER STAGE

What: Tampa Theatre

Where: 711 N. Franklin St., Tampa

Cost: Given the variety of films, events, and live performance, pricing varies.

Pro Tip: Seating on the orchestral level was expanded recently to give visitors an extra half foot of leg room—those 1926 theatre seats can be a little bit tight.

to the projector room. Fink keeps company with the spirit of doorman Robert Green Lanier, who has the distinction of being the only person known to have died at the theatre, from a suspicious second-floor fall. You might also encounter a lady in white believed to be the victim of a carriage accident on the land where the theatre was built.

WINTER'S TAIL

How did efforts to save an injured dolphin change the field of prosthetics?

The prognosis was grim for the young dolphin named Winter that had been rescued from a crab trap on December 10, 2005. Despite the efforts of the team at Clearwater Marine Aquarium, Winter's tail did not heal and eventually detached from her body. If Winter was going to survive and thrive, she would need an innovative solution.

Enter prosthetist Kevin Carroll and his team. After 18 months of research, development, and testing, they produced a unique plastic and silicone tail. To prevent chafing and irritation, the team also put a soft gel-like sleeve over the tail stump.

The team's efforts were successful and became the subject of a book and a popular film, *Dolphin Tale*, starring Morgan Freeman, Harry Connick Jr., and

RESCUED

What: Winter the Dolphin

Where: Clearwater Marine Aquarium, 249 Windward Passage, Clearwater

Cost: Adults, $24.95; children ages 3–12, $19.95; seniors, $22.95. For a bit more, the aquarium offers packages and animal experiences.

Pro Tip: If you find a dolphin, whale, sea turtle, or river otter in distress in the Tampa Bay area, call the Emergency Stranding Hotline at 727-441-1790 Ext.1

Technically proficient: the CMA can perform on-site lab procedures such as blood cell counts, hematocrits (PCV), cytology, blood glucose, fecal sample analysis, and gastric sample salinity testing.

You can see how Winter's prosthetic tail has improved over time and watch as she is fit with the most current version.

Ashley Judd. Today Winter is alive and well, receiving star treatment at the Clearwater Marine Aquarium, along with Hope, a fellow dolphin who starred in the sequel, *Dolphin Tale 2*.

Winter's story didn't end with prosthetics just for dolphins. Carroll, who had developed the gel-sleeve for Winter's tail, applied the same approach to helping ease the pain of an Iraq War veteran who had lost both legs in a mortar attack. Based on the results, the approach has since been adopted as a standard practice worldwide.

Clearwater Marine Aquarium continues its mission of public education and research, as well as rescuing, rehabilitating, and releasing sick and injured marine animals. It is currently in the process of building a major addition to its facility that will provide more space for the care of turtles, manatees, dolphins, and other sea creatures.

EVERY DAY I'M SHUFFLING

Have any sports ever been invented in Florida?

With beautiful weather year round and a slew of sports teams (including the Buccaneers, the Lightning, the Rays, and the Rowdies), golf courses, gyms, and fitness centers just about everywhere you look, it's hardly surprising that Tampa ranks consistently near the top of most lists of America's best cities for active lifestyles. But of all the sports to make a comeback and draw a hip, young crowd, would you have guessed that it would be shuffleboard?

The exact origins of the game are a bit murky—it may have evolved from similar games in England like shovel-penny. The modern version was introduced around 1913 in Daytona Beach and then formalized in St. Petersburg, where the game was officially defined in 1924, the court size was standardized in 1928, and the National Shuffleboard Association was formed in 1931.

St. Pete has remained at the forefront of the sport as its popularity has ebbed and flowed over the years. Lately it's been on the rise again, and since the St. Petersburg Shuffleboard Club started its free Friday nights in 2005, which are open to the public, it has seen its membership swell to over 1,200 members, thus ensuring that it will remain the world's largest shuffleboard club for the foreseeable future.

Regulation shuffleboard court dimensions are 52 feet from end to end, 39 feet from baseline to baseline, and six feet in width.

2024 will mark St. Pete Shuffleboard Club's 100th anniversary; it is as popular today as ever.

The success of the club has inspired several bars and restaurants to install courts. In 2018 Tampa Heights became the first neighborhood with an indoor court, and Clearwater has long been home to the USA National Shuffleboard Association Hall of Fame, which inducts new members each year in the categories of Player Awards and Special Awards.

RIDING THE RAIL

What: St. Petersburg Shuffleboard Club

Where: 599 Mirror Lake Dr. N., St. Petersburg

Cost: Individual membership, $35 annually; family membership, $60 annually; Friday nights, free (BYOB)

Pro Tip: If you're new to the game, check out the monthly Beginner Boot Camp at the St. Petersburg Shuffleboard Club, where you can learn to shuffle for just $10.

THE LEGENDARY PINK PALACE

If Jay Gatsby had been a snowbird, where would he have spent his winters?

Few places in Tampa Bay so perfectly preserve the prosperity of the Roaring Twenties as the iconic Don CeSar hotel. Sometimes likened to a giant pink birthday cake, it has returned from the brink of destruction more than once.

Thomas Rowe opened his beloved hotel to the public in 1928, hosting a veritable who's who of high society at the time, including F. Scott Fitzgerald and Clarence Darrow. Rowe managed to keep the hotel afloat through the Depression, thanks largely to a three-year contract with the New York Yankees.

Following Rowe's death in 1940, control of the hotel passed to his estranged wife. Without Rowe's almost preternatural business sense, the hotel quickly found itself in financial trouble. Its salvation came in the form of the US Army, which converted into a convalescent center for WWII airmen. Following this, it served as the regional VA office and recreation center before again heading into decline.

In 1972 William Bowman became the new owner and committed over $3 million to restoration. And the pink palace was reborn as a hotel and a popular location for filming. You can see it in films such as *Once Upon a Time in America*, *Forever Mine*,

---

Another vintage hotel that's undergone a transformation in recent years is the Vinoy in St. Petersburg. It offers a popular combination of tour and brunch.

The Don CeSar has managed to survive and stay in style for nearly a century.

PRETTY IN PINK

What: The Don CeSar

Where: 3400 Gulf Blvd., St. Pete Beach

Cost: Check the hotel's website for room rates and availability.

Pro Tip: If you're looking for a superior, upscale dining experience, check out the Maritana Grille inside the hotel.

and *The Infiltrator*, as well as in television shows like *Thunder in Paradise* and *Emeril's Florida*. The famous and infamous, from Bill Gates to O. J. Simpson, have been spotted there.

It also has its fair share of guests who allegedly never checked out and still haunt the old ballroom and hallways. Some are seen wearing 1920s attire, while others are clad in military uniforms. Rowe himself is said to make an occasional visit, perhaps to make sure that his one true love is still the belle of the beach.

THE OTHER BRITISH INVASION OF FLORIDA

How did a massive trove of Beatles memorabilia come to be displayed in Dunedin?

It's true that the British temporarily wrested control of Florida from the Spanish before it became the 27th state in the United States, but that's not the British invasion you'll learn about at the Penny Lane Beatles Museum.

Despite sharing a name with that of a Beatles song, long-time Dunedin resident "Doctor Robert" Entel did not set out with the intention of acquiring a museum's worth of memorabilia. He took his first step down that road as a medical student in London, when he purchased a few Beatles pins from a street vendor outside of his dorm.

From there he slowly began to amass a unique and impressive collection, which he estimates to contain as many as 1,200 pieces—about half of which are currently on display at the museum inside of Stirling Art Studios & Gallery. Just two years after opening, the museum is already considering a potential expansion.

The collection includes everything from autographs, buttons, cake toppers, gumball machines, concert posters, dishware, and other mass-marketed items to far more unusual and one-of-a-kind items. This latter category includes an original pair of Prada sunglasses worn by John Lennon, which he gave to a friend, as they

---

If you visit on a weekday, look for curator Colin Bissett who can tell you about growing up in Liverpool and watching the Beatles perform at small venues prior to their meteoric rise to superstardom.

Along the figurative path from Penny Lane to Abby Road, there's now a very literal stop in Dunedin, FL.

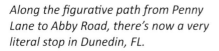

STEP INSIDE, LOVE

What: Penny Lane Beatles Museum

Where: 730 Broadway, Second Floor, Dunedin

Cost: Admission is free.

Pro Tip: The museum will reopen in the fall of 2020. For more information you can call (727) 281-8130.

were not his usual prescription, and his TWA travel razor and a pair of his long johns, which came to be part of the collection through Yoko Ono's second husband. There's also a serape worn by Paul McCartney that arrived via Jane Asher, to whom he was once engaged, but never married.

Both diehard fans of the Fab Four and those who may be unfamiliar with the global Beatlemania phenomenon will enjoy a stroll through Penny Lane.

A BURNING QUESTION

Do people ever just burst into flames for no apparent reason?

For most residents of St. Petersburg, July 1, 1951, began as a typical day. "Most residents," however, does not include Mrs. Pansy Carpenter. She was first awakened around five in the morning by the smell of smoke, but she assumed that it was just an overheated water pump. A few hours later, when she went to deliver a letter to her tenant Mary Reeser, she found the door handle hot to the touch and went to find help. When Mrs. Carpenter and her neighbors forced open the door, what they found was both horrifying and inexplicable.

There on an easy chair in the corner was a pile of ash that had just the night before been 67-year-old Mary Reeser. Oddly, the fire seemed to be extremely localized—so much so that one of Reeser's feet, still in a slipper, was unscathed. The heat was intense enough to have shrunk Reeser's skull the size of a soda can, yet there was minimal damage to the rest of the apartment.

The leading theory came to be the exceptionally rare phenomenon known as spontaneous human combustion (SHC), which is described as a chemical reaction inside the body that causes it to burst into flames without any external source of ignition. Another potential explanation was the "wick effect," in

---

Mary Reeser is not the only suspected SHC victim. In his book *Ablaze!* author Larry E. Arnold suggests that there have been hundreds of similar reports from all over the world over the course of three centuries.

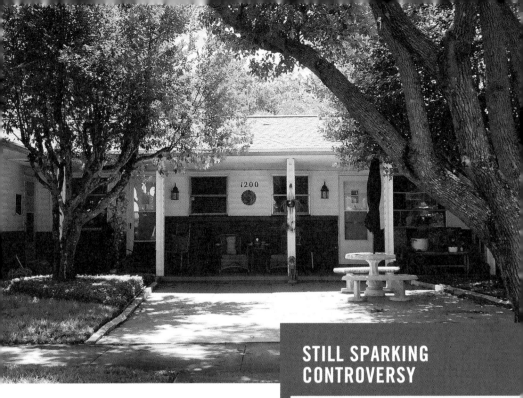

Today the former residence of Mary Reeser shows no signs of what is still one of Tampa Bay's most bizarre and unsolved mysteries.

STILL SPARKING CONTROVERSY

What: The former home of Mary Reeser

Where: Cherry St. NE, St. Petersburg

Cost: Free to drive or stroll past.

Pro Tip: Today the location is private property and not open to the public—be respectful and don't pester the residents, who may or may not be aware of what once transpired there.

which the body's own fat can feed an intense, localized fire like a candle. Other suggestions included ball lightning, Tesla-styled death rays, and, of course, extraterrestrials.

Detectives settled on a statement simply that Reeser was the victim of an "accidental death by fire of unknown origin." Given that the case is now almost 70 years old, it's likely that we will never know anything more definitive than that.

ONE OF US! ONE OF US!

Is there really an entire community of circus sideshow performers in Florida?

Heading south of Tampa on US Highway 41 about 80 years ago, you might have stopped in the small town of Gibsonton—"Gibtown" to the locals—to buy some fruit from the stand run by Siamese twin sisters. There you could also find Al "The Giant" Tomani and his wife, Jeanie "The Half Woman," managing a campsite, bakeshop, and local fire department. For food or drink, you could pop into the local restaurant and see specially designed chairs for what today we might call extraordinarily plus-sized individuals. You could mail a postcard from what at the time was the only post office with a counter for dwarves and small people. In its heyday, Gibsonton was home to some of the most famous sideshow performers in the world and a refuge from a public that was far less sensitive to deformities and special needs.

Today, though, Gibsonton looks pretty much like any other Gulf Coast community. With the decline and closure of circuses and sideshows, you won't see carnival rides and exotic animal pens on the residents' lawns (although local zoning laws still permit it). At Showtown Bar & Restaurant you have a better chance of finding lobster tacos than the Lobster Boy.

If you really want to explore the town's carny past though, you can visit the International Independent Showmen's Association

---

Gibsonton has provided a unique setting for multiple books and television shows, including the X-Files episode "Humbug," about alleged Fiji mermaid attacks, which guest-starred The Enigma and Jim Rose of the Jim Rose Circus Sideshow.

The International Independent Showman's Museum preserves the niche entertainment industry for which Gibsonton is best known.

CARNYVILLE, USA

What: Gibsonton

Where: 6938 Riverview Dr., Riverview, FL

Cost: Free to wander the neighborhood. Admission to the International Independent Showmen's Museum is $12 for adults and $7 for students with ID.

Pro Tip: Even though the number of carnival and sideshow performers has dwindled significantly, the residents do still appreciate their privacy, so be mindful when you visit.

and Museum, which features antique equipment, billboards, one of the first Ferris wheels in the United States, and plenty of other vintage Americana. You can also find digital photos and oral histories through the University of South Florida's Special Collections or head further south to the Ringling Museum for big-name big-top artifacts and history.

THE WARLOCK OF WESLEY CHAPEL

Was artist Lewis VanDercar a sorcerer, a creative prankster, or maybe both?

Why is it that Tampa Bay seems like a beacon for renegade artists and do-it-yourselfers who carve thousands of miniature circus figures, build their own metal castles, and turn their homes into giant mosaic artworks? We may never know, but at least we can marvel at what they summon forth into being.

When it comes to the confluence of creativity and conjuration, few individuals can compare to artist, sculptor, and self-proclaimed magus Lewis VanDercar. In 1973 he moved to the quiet Quail Hollow neighborhood (now Wesley Chapel), where he constructed his own dome-shaped home, studio, and sculpture garden populated with mythical beasts. He worked at this location until his death in 1988. On Friday nights he hosted open houses for friends, fellow artists, mystics, metaphysicians, and curiosity seekers.

Originally from Detroit, VanDercar served in the US Navy before becoming an animator for the *Popeye the Sailor* cartoon. He returned to the open seas during World War II with the Merchant Marines and also did a stint as an aircraft engineer before settling in Miami and doing odd jobs.

Upon discovering that he could support himself as a full-time artist, he converted his home into a studio and European-styled

---

Sadly, one of VanDercar's best-known local creations, the 60-foot-long fire-breathing Annie the Dragon, which gave Dragon Point its name, was destroyed during a storm in 2002.

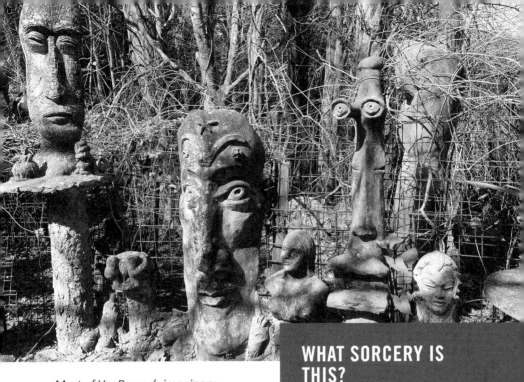

Most of VanDercar's imaginary creatures are more playful than terrifying.

WHAT SORCERY IS THIS?

What: The Warlock House Enchantment–VanDercar Studios

Where: 25950 Queen Sago Pl., Wesley Chapel

Cost: Free

Pro Tip: If you want to visit the property, you'll need to reach out and coordinate through the Warlock House's Facebook page.

salon frequented by both artists and occultists. He also embraced his inner Andy Kaufman, which resulted in antics such as trying to sell his pet poltergeist via classified ad and hosting a gathering at a nearby park to witness the arrival of an extinct primitive bird, which never materialized.

Today, "The Warlock's House" is home to VanDercar's daughter, grandson, and granddaughter-in-law. That the garden has overrun his artworks only enhances the sense of having stumbled upon some forgotten pagan ritual site. Currently, machinations are underway to reawaken whatever magic lies dormant there as a new creative space.

THEY PAVED PARADISE AND PUT UP A PARKING LOT

Who is Mother Meres and why is she featured in a mosaic mural in Tarpon Springs?

In 1882 Amelia Petzold Meres and her husband, Walter, joined other early settlers in what is now Tarpon Springs. Born in Germany and brought to the country as a five-year-old, Amelia became a trained florist and gardener. Walter ran a bunkhouse called the Tropical, while Amelia provided the fresh vegetables and fruit for guests from her garden. She brought flowers to the sick and provided bouquets and floral decorations for all occasions, which earned her the nickname "Mother Meres." She was the first to plant trees along the streets of Tarpon Springs and the cycads at the now aptly named Cycadia Cemetery.

As Walter's health declined, Mother Meres took over the operation and renamed their boardinghouse the Ferns Hotel. Following her own death on October 20, 1923, the garden she left to the city was made into a Victorian-styled park along Pinellas Avenue. Her name was inscribed on an urn provided by the Garden Club and benches were placed under the shade of palms. By the 1950s, though, the city was growing fast and turned most of the park into a parking lot. And so, it seemed, the legacy and green thumbprints of this pioneering local humanitarian might fade.

Meres Park was not the only local landmark to end up as a parking lot. The much-loved, over-the-top Polynesian tourist attraction Tiki Gardens in Indian Shores met with a similar fate.

The Garden Fairies applied their creativity to ensure that Mother Meres will not be forgotten.

Enter the Garden Fairies, a group of creative and civic-minded local women on a mission to enhance and create new gardens. Of the dozen impressive projects they have undertaken, creating the largescale mural of Mother Meres is their best known. It was completed on October 20, 2010—exactly 84 years after the death of Mother Meres. By either coincidence or garden fairy magic, her great-grandson happened to be in town the weekend the mural was unveiled.

GREEN THUMBPRINTS

What: Mother Meres Mural

Where: Pinellas Ave. between E. Tarpon Ave. and E. Court St., Tarpon Springs

Cost: Free

Pro Tip: If you feel inspired to do some gardening after visiting the mural, check out The Garden and the Relic just down the street.

CAN I GET AN AMEN?

Who is the most famous graduate of the Florida Bible Institute in Tampa's Temple Terrace neighborhood?

Over the course of his career, Reverend Billy Graham conducted 417 crusades in 185 countries and territories on six different continents, reaching over 200 million individuals. He preached alongside Martin Luther King Jr. in 1957, met with countless world leaders, and served as spiritual advisor to multiple presidents, including Truman and Obama, all of which made him one of the most influential Christian leaders in modern times.

But that Billy Graham is far different from the teenager who transferred to the Florida Bible Institute in 1937 after barely making it through his first semester at Bob Jones College in Greenville, SC.

It was here that Graham claims to have found his true calling "on the 18th green of the Temple Terrace Golf and Country Club," which was next to the Bible Institute campus. He was known to take a canoe across the Hillsborough River to a small island, where he would hone his preaching skills. It's unclear whether he convinced any of the birds, fish, and alligators there to accept Jesus Christ as their personal savior, but he became confident enough to deliver his first sermon at Bostwick Baptist Church near Palatka, FL, while he was still a student.

Depression-era Tampa offered more than wildlife to preach to, so Graham decided to start at the intersection of Franklin and Fortune Streets, where the jobless and homeless looked for work.

Billy Graham isn't the only evangelist to have called Tampa home—Rodney Howard-Browne, pastor of The River at Tampa Bay, has lived in the area since the mid-1990s.

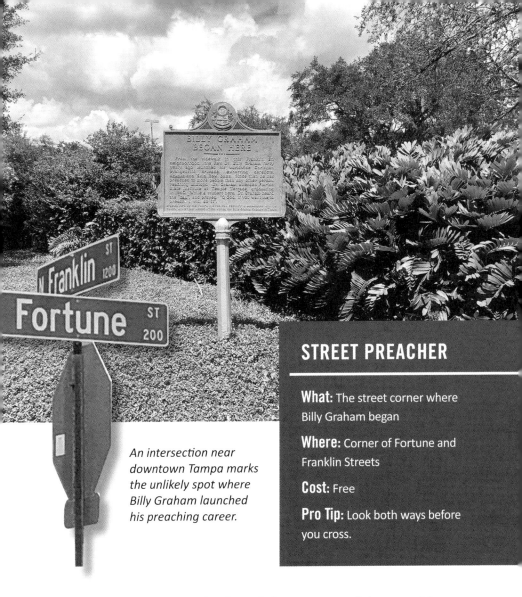

BILLY GRAHAM
BEGAN HERE

An intersection near downtown Tampa marks the unlikely spot where Billy Graham launched his preaching career.

STREET PREACHER

What: The street corner where Billy Graham began

Where: Corner of Fortune and Franklin Streets

Cost: Free

Pro Tip: Look both ways before you cross.

And in trying to change the fate of these poor and downtrodden souls, Graham also shaped his own. Today you can see a historical marker at the intersection, which marks it as the spot where Billy Graham began his career and launched his worldwide ministry.

LEFT FOR DEAD

How did the Second Seminole War begin?

We can only speculate on the first thing that passed through Major Francis Langhorne Dade's mind on December 28, 1835, as he led two companies of soldiers on a resupply mission from Fort Brooke, now Tampa, to Fort King, near Ocala. Maybe it was relief, as he and his men had already passed safely across the two rivers where he thought Seminoles, under pressure from the US government to relocate, were most likely to attack. We know that the last thing to pass through Dade's head that afternoon was a bullet fired personally by Chief Micanopy when 180 Seminoles ambushed the troops roughly 25 miles south of their destination. Surprised and outgunned, the soldiers were slaughtered in what became known as the Dade Massacre and what most historians consider the beginning of the Second Seminole War.

Of the 110 soldiers, only three survived the initial attack. One of those three, Private Edward Decourcey, was cut down trying to make his escape. That left Private Joseph Sprague and Private Ransom Clark.

Of the two remaining survivors, Clark seemed to be in the worse shape, having been shot five times. Still, no doubt in excruciating pain, he managed to make his way slowly back to Fort Brooke, 50 miles away. Pursued by Seminoles on horseback and on foot while also avoiding the snakes, gators, and other dangerous denizens of the swamp, Clark collapsed within a mile of the fort. If not for the help of a friendly Indian woman, he almost certainly would have

---

While you're visiting the Tampa Bay History Center, don't miss the short film (with animatronics) about Osceola and the Seminole Wars.

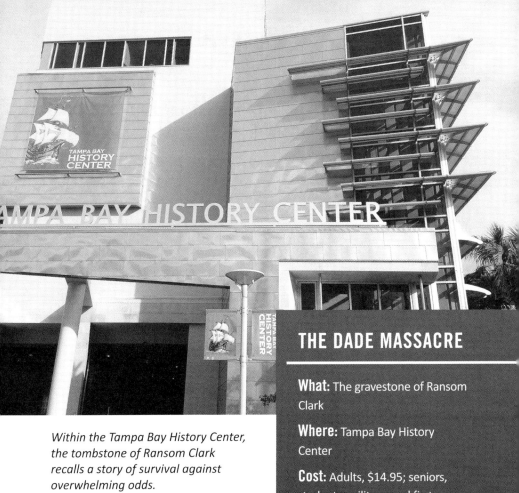

Within the Tampa Bay History Center, the tombstone of Ransom Clark recalls a story of survival against overwhelming odds.

THE DADE MASSACRE

What: The gravestone of Ransom Clark

Where: Tampa Bay History Center

Cost: Adults, $14.95; seniors, students, military, and first responders, $12.95; youth ages 7–17, $10.95; members and children ages 6 and under, free

Pro Tip: If you work up an appetite, there's a Columbia Café conveniently located right there in the same building.

perished there. But instead he beat the extraordinary odds to warn his fellow soldiers, providing the only account from the US side of events. Today you can find his tombstone in the Tampa Bay History Center.

FORM AND FUNCTION

Did an argument between an architect and a priest result in a distinctly churchlike public bathroom?

Most travelers know that finding a clean, public bathroom can be a challenge. But every once in a while you might discover one that is truly outstanding, like the Bryant Park bathroom in New York, with its fresh flowers, art, and classical music, or the award-winning Hermitage Hotel Men's Room in Nashville. And if you're in St. Petersburg at the corner of Second Avenue and Bayshore Drive, then you have the exceedingly good fortune to be in front of Comfort Station One.

As the Sunshine City grew, it knew the value of keeping tourists comfortable. This led, in 1927, to constructing a public restroom. The work was awarded to Henry Taylor, known for creating other landmark buildings such as the Vinoy Hotel. He decided on a distinctive octagonal design in Romanesque Revival style with multicolored bricks and a domed tile roof.

The similarity between Comfort Station One and St. Mary's Church is not a coincidence—Taylor was the architect on both projects. There's a tale that a dispute over payment for his work on the church led Taylor to use the same design for the bathroom, but this is clearly false, as the bathroom was built two years before the church. The bathroom was, however, likely a prototype for the church.

Comfort Station One is not the area's only restroom to receive national attention. The J.N. Ding Darling National Wildlife Refuge in Sanibel was recognized as "America's Best Bathroom" in 2018 by Cintas.

Comfort Station One was featured in the February 1929 issue of The American City.

There's another story about one luckless individual for whom Comfort Station One offers no relief . . . or escape. Her name is Agnes, and she is the 1930s-era ghost reputed to haunt the ladies' side of the building. There are numerous accounts of cold spots, mirrors fogging up, lights flickering, muttering, and even pleasant conversation . . . coming from an empty stall. It's unclear how she came to spend her afterlife in a public restroom, but she doesn't seem overly troubled by it.

THE BIGGEST LITTLE TRAIN IN TAMPA BAY

Are there any train stops in Largo?

The sun may have long set on most of the major railroad lines that made Tampa Bay what it is today, but there's one recent railroad that's been steadily growing in popularity. Still, you might not have heard of Largo Central Railroad before—maybe it's because it consists of just about a mile and a half of tracks and the only stop along its route is inside Largo Central Park. Or perhaps it's the schedule that has kept this miniature marvel something a hidden gem for more than 25 years. The train runs only from 10 a.m. to 4 p.m. Saturdays and Sundays of the first full weekend of each month.

The painstakingly accurate, one-eighth scale locomotive models are run and maintained by a growing group of volunteers (numbering now over 100), many of whom have experience as conductors or engineers on full-sized railroads. The track winds around a corner of the park, past a waterfall pond and through a

ALL ABOARD

What: Largo Central Railroad

Where: 101 Central Park Dr., Largo

Cost: Free on the first full weekend of the month; $125 per hour for private rentals

Pro Tip: You can save time by filling out the waiver ahead of time online.

Largo Central Park isn't just dog friendly—it actually celebrates some four-legged heroes with a small memorial to the Largo Police Department canines.

The track gets seasonal makeovers in October and December each year for Halloween and Christmas.

tunnel. As one of just six or so such tracks in Florida, it is popular not only with the locals but also with occasional visiting dignitaries. It's not uncommon for there to be a bit of a wait, since Largo Central Railroad sees over 1,300 riders on an average weekend. If you would rather have it all to yourself, it's available for birthday parties and other events every second or fourth weekend of the month.

BURIED TREASURE

Are there riches hidden below the soil of Central Florida?

If you want to find real buried treasure in Florida, leave your metal detector at the beach and head inland about an hour from Tampa to the Mulberry Phosphate Museum.

Phosphate rock is a major driver of Florida's economy. It is used primarily to create phosphate fertilizers, which can increase crop yields and health. Roughly 75 percent of the phosphate used by farmers and gardeners in the United States comes from mines in the Bone Valley region of Central Florida.

The Mulberry Phosphate Museum consists of three primary galleries. The first of these, located inside a converted boxcar, is Phosphate Gallery, which provides information about the industry, including what phosphate is, how it's mined and processed, and how it benefits the local community and economy. The second gallery, in an adjacent boxcar, is the Historic Railroad Gallery, which illuminates the connection between the phosphate mining industry, the birth and growth of the town, and the railroads that enabled Mulberry to supply the rest of the state and country.

The third and largest gallery is housed in the former railroad depot. In 1985 it became home to a prehistoric fossil collection acquired from the Bone Valley Fossil Collection in Bradley. Virtually all the fossils on display represent native animals that once

---

It's worth mentioning that over issues like environmental impact, the relationship between the mines and local communities can get a bit more complicated than the adorable cartoon saber-toothed tiger mascot might let on.

The Historic Railroad Gallery explores how life in Mulberry has changed over the years and includes a mining company store display.

DEPOSITS AND WITHDRAWALS

What: Mulberry Phosphate Museum

Where: 101 SE First St., Mulberry

Cost: Admission is free; donations are appreciated.

Pro Tip: The museum is open from 9 a.m. to 5 p.m. Tuesday through Saturday and closed on Sunday and Monday.

inhabited the region, including some that might surprise you, like camels and rhinoceroses.

The museum also has a few outdoor exhibits, including a massive dragline bucket, a fossil dig for aspiring young paleontologists, a preserved rail car, and the most recent acquisition: a Manchester locomotive from the 1880s.

WHERE THE SIDEWALK (NEVER) ENDS

Does Bayshore Boulevard have the longest sidewalk in the world?

Stretching 4.5 miles with spectacular views of the bay, the skyline, historic homes, and the pirate ship *Jose Gasparilla*, Bayshore Boulevard is one of Tampa's most memorable roads. Starting at Ballast Point, which was the site of the city's first trolley line, it winds its way north through the historic Hyde Park neighborhood and past Columbus Statue Park.

While many are familiar with the fitness stations along the way and the 15 cast-bronze trail markers at half mile, kilometer, and mile—which collectively form Michele Oka Doner's artwork *Winged Figure: From the Firmament*—there are also plenty of more obscure points of interest along the way. Just north of West Platt Street is a propeller-topped monument commemorating Tony Jannus and the world's first scheduled airline flight from St. Petersburg to Tampa. Further

WALK IT OFF

What: Bayshore Boulevard

Where: North along Tampa Bay from Ballast Point Park

Cost: Free

Pro Tip: Bayshore Boulevard is a busy street, so be mindful of cars, as well as bikers, runners, rollerbladers, and others.

Ballast Point Park at the northern end of Bayshore Boulevard was previously called Jules Verne Park, despite the author never having lived in or visited Tampa Bay.

Bayshore Boulevard may not be the longest sidewalk in America, but it is home to plenty of noteworthy monuments hiding in plain sight.

south along the inner sidewalk is a memorial to Tampa Bay's Scottish settlers, the base of which is set with a stone taken from beside the Wallace Yew tree in William Wallace's hometown of Elderslie, Scotland.

But is Bayshore really the longest continuous sidewalk in the world, as some claim? No, it is not. That title likely belongs to the Rambla in Montevideo, Uruguay, with a length of 13.7 miles. What about the United States, then? Surely Bayshore Boulevard must be America's longest uninterrupted sidewalk, right? Well, no, technically, that's probably not true either. The southern side of Seawall Boulevard in Galveston, TX, holds that record with a sidewalk length of 10.3 miles.

In that case, some might ask, shouldn't we all stop referring to Bayshore Boulevard as the longest sidewalk in the world or in the United States? To which, one imagines, the city might respond, "Quick, look over there! Dolphins!"

SEA COW SANCTUARY

Where, outside of an aquarium, are you most likely to see a manatee in the Tampa Bay area?

Usually when we hear stories about the impact of human development along the coast, they are predictably tales of displaced animals and lost habitats. Every once in a while, though, mankind has the exact opposite effect, inadvertently benefiting the local flora and fauna.

Such is the case with Tampa Electric's Big Bend Power Station Unit 4 in Apollo Beach. In 1986, when Unit 4 began commercial operation, local residents started noticing a large and growing number of manatees floating in the discharge canal, where warm, clean salt water flows back out from the power station. When the waters of Tampa Bay drop to 68 degrees, manatees typically head south, seeking warmer water

With manatees coming to enjoy the warm water and people coming to watch the manatees, the Manatee Viewing Center (MVC) was a logical development.

SEASONAL VISITORS

What: Apollo Beach Manatee Viewing Center

Where: 6990 Dickman Rd., Apollo Beach

Cost: Free

Pro Tip: Open daily from 10 a.m. to 5 p.m. from November to mid-April.

It's easy to confuse manatees with their relatives, dugongs. While both are herbivorous sea mammals of the Sirenian order, you can tell them apart by their tails, snouts, and location—dugongs are native to the Indo-West Pacific.

The warm water discharged by TECO's Big Bend powerplant makes for a Manatee-friendly environment.

The MVC, named a state and federally designated manatee sanctuary in 2002, marked its 34th season in 2019. In addition to providing safety from the cold for manatees, there is a 50-foot-tall viewing tower along a nature path and a boardwalk that stretches out from under a canopy of mangrove trees.

Each season, which runs from November first through April 15, about 300,000 humans visit the MVC, and on a good day you might see well over 100 manatees. You'll also find a touch tank with horseshoe crabs and cownose rays, as well as a butterfly garden.

THE BIRTHPLACE OF DEATH METAL

How did Tampa become the capital of death metal?

It may seem counterintuitive that Tampa, with its reputation as a quiet, sleepy city, would become the epicenter of an extreme heavy metal subgenre, but it's true, nonetheless.

Heavy metal came onto the music scene in the late 1960s, pioneered by bands such as Black Sabbath, Led Zeppelin, Iron Maiden, and others. As a subgenre, death metal is characterized by low-tuned guitars, morbid and occult lyrics, and a number of other hallmarks, including abrupt tempo, atonality, and intensely aggressive drumming. As far as which death metal band was "the first," Death, formed in Orlando in 1983, is a strong contender.

A short drive west of Orlando, brothers Jim and Tom Morris opened their own studio, Morrisound Recording, in Temple Terrace in 1981. By 1985 they had outgrown their first storefront and moved into the first and only facility on Florida's Gulf Coast designed specifically for audio recording, located on 56th Street in north Tampa. It was here that the Morrises produced a demo album for Xecutioner (which later changed its name to Obituary) in 1984, establishing themselves and Tampa as critical players in the nascent heavy metal offshoot.

Following its work for Xecutioner, Morrisound produced albums for Morbid Angel and others, including Death's 1988 album Leprosy.

Morrisound's original studio became home to the Tampa-based rock juggernaut Trans-Siberian Orchestra.

A quiet, unassuming building in Temple Terrace belies the musical maelstrom often raging within.

ROCK ME ASMODEUS

What: Morrisound Recording

Where: 8003 N. Ninth St., Tampa

Cost: Free to visit from outside; recording session costs vary.

Pro Tip: If you're looking for a studio tour, you can email your request to info@ morrisound.com.

The company's technical prowess also earned it some big-name, mainstream clients, such as Ozzy Osbourne, Robert Plant, Third Eye Blind, and Little Feat.

In 2014 the brothers sold their facility and contemplated their next iteration. In 2018 they found their new home in Tampa's Sulphur Springs neighborhood. Here, furnished with brand new, state-of-the-art equipment, they will no doubt continue to refine and produce a unique style of sonic fury worthy of any malevolent deity.

BLESSED BE THE WINDOWS OF THE SEMINOLE FINANCE CO.

Have religious images ever appeared unexpectedly in Tampa Bay?

If you're familiar with the phrase "seeing is believing," then consider for a moment if the inverse might also be true—that believing can be seeing, whether it's the face of Jesus on a tortilla; the hoofprint of Muhammad's steed, Burāq, on a sacred rock; or, in this particular case, an image of the Virgin Mary across the exterior windows of a local business.

Clearwater Virgin Mary was first spotted on December 17, 1996, just off US Highway 19 North in Clearwater. A stain roughly 60 feet tall by 20 feet wide appeared across six large panes of glass looking out over the parking lot of what at the time was the Seminole Finance Company (and which has since become Our Lady of Clearwater).

The window image received international media attention, making it a sudden and unexpected pilgrimage destination, with as many as half a million visitors just in the first month. Some remain convinced that they witnessed a miracle, despite a very plausible scientific explanation—namely, corrosion of the metallic coating on the glass.

Nearby St. Nicholas Greek Orthodox Cathedral in Tarpon Springs is home to another unusual religious phenomenon—the painting known as "The Weeping Icon of Saint Nicholas," which was last observed to shed tears on December 8, 1973.

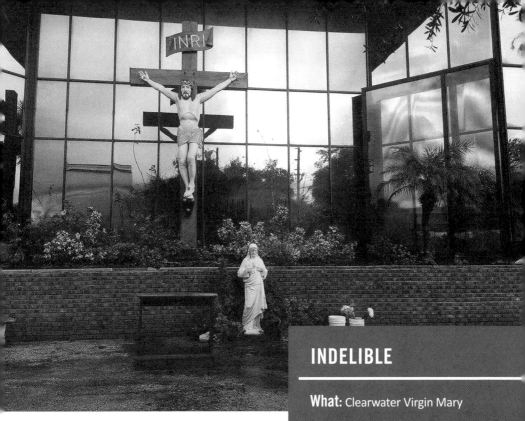

A small shrine has been erected in front of the remaining window panels.

The parking lot became the site of an annual celebration for the Virgin of Guadalupe, but gradually regular visitors to the site tapered off by the early 2000s. In 2004, a local slingshot-wielding teenager vandalized the windows, shattering the top three, which composed the head of the image. The lower three panels were preserved under bulletproof glass the following year.

Today if you visit the building, the stain on the lower three panels is still clearly visible. While it no longer draws the massive crowds that it once did, some still stop by from time to time for meditation and prayer.

BRADEN CASTLE RUINS

What are those old stone ruins doing in the middle of a mobile home community?

There's not much left of the once stately home that brothers Hector and Dr. Joseph Addison Braden built in the 1840s—mostly crumbling, overgrown stonework behind a fence in a small park . . . and the name, which was adopted by Bradenton.

The brothers moved to the area from Tallahassee to take advantage of the Armed Occupation Act of 1842, which provided generous portions of cheap land to anyone willing to defend it from the local Seminoles and thereby push them further from their land.

The brothers built their two-story "castle" primarily using tabby (a mixture of crushed oyster shell, lime, water, and sand) on the 1,100 acres they had acquired to raise sugar cane. They survived storms and fended off a Seminole attack in 1856, but shortly thereafter, Hector passed away and the following year their crops were ruined by corn borers. Like other plantations in the area, the Braden estate sank deeper into debt until Dr. Braden returned north to the Florida Panhandle.

But the story of Braden Castle didn't end there.

Left to decay for over 70 years, the structure was rediscovered in the 1920s by the "tin can tourists" who came south in search of adventure in their Model T Fords. The Castle became a local landmark and around it went up tents and cottages, eventually

---

If you want to see what Braden Castle looked like in its heyday, you can find some photos and other items of local historical interest at the Bishop Museum of Science and Nature.

Braden Castle, 1890

Built by Col. Joseph Braden in the mid 1800s, the castle was occupied by the Braden family until destroyed by fire in 1904. It was built of tabby, a native material made

LEGACY OF THE BROTHERS BRADEN

What: Braden Castle Park

Where: At the intersection of Braden Castle Dr. and Plaza St. E. in Bradenton

Cost: Free

Pro Tip: The roads through the community are a bit windy and confusing—if you can find Braden Castle Drive, just stay on that until you reach the park.

Braden Castle endured Seminole attacks, fires, storms, and other hardships.

incorporated as the Camping Tourists of America. By the 1930s there was a small but thriving community. In the '50s the town of Manatee was absorbed into Bradenton, and Braden Castle Park was officially recognized as a unique historical district in 1985.

Today, 180 years since its construction, fragments of the Braden brothers' home still jut upward like broken teeth from a grudge match between a government and an indigenous people.

BODIES IN MOTION

Don't you need to be in peak physical condition to learn circus arts like aerial silk and acrobatics?

Brought together initially by their passion for partner acrobatics, Jessica DeLeo and Aaron Tremper shared a bolder, longer-term vision—to bring together under one roof world-class instructors delivering all levels of training in circus arts, from acrobatics to jiu jitsu, flexibility, object manipulation, and more. That vision became reality when, just three years ago, a warehouse space in St. Pete that was the former home of an art collective became available. Thus was born The Movement Sanctuary—a hybrid training gym, event space, and celebration of the myriad forms of human motion.

In the short time that The Movement Sanctuary has been open, it has been both a figurative and literal whirlwind of activity. Whereas previously the more esoteric physical forms of art, such as circus sphere wheel and hand balancing had been largely siloed and were inaccessible to beginners and novices, today you can register for as many as 60 different classes. While DeLeo and Tremper work as two of the permanent trainers, they host visiting instructors from around the world with credentials that include performing with Cirque du Soleil and other big-name troupes.

According to DeLeo and contrary to popular belief, you don't need to have a partner, be an endurance athlete or have any extra joints in your body to get started. The Movement Sanctuary offers many beginner-level classes, and any given class might

---

If you're looking for another meditative form of motion, drop by the headquarters of the Taoist Tai Chi Society of the USA, located in Dunedin.

The Movement Sanctuary provides all the space, equipment, and training you need to get started in circus arts.

IN THE FLOW

What: The Movement Sanctuary

Where: 910 Fifth Ave. N., Unit A, St. Petersburg

Cost: Drop-in rates, $20 per class; open training, $15

Pro Tip: A variety of class packs are available and offer some savings in terms of the per-class cost.

have participants ranging from elementary school students to senior citizens.

The Movement Sanctuary has been embraced by the local creative community, and not surprisingly, the DJ parties they've hosted in the past are the stuff of legends. They have since scaled back their event schedule a bit, but you can still attend their ecstatic First Saturday dances.

CHILDREN OF THE SUN

Is there an entire college campus designed by Frank Lloyd Wright just east of Tampa?

When you think of a Frank Lloyd Wright building, is it Fallingwater in Mill Run, PA? The Guggenheim in New York? The Robie House in Chicago?

What about virtually all the buildings on the Florida Southern College campus—also known as Wright's Child of the Sun? Did this location come to mind for you? If not, it probably should—it's the single-largest cluster of his buildings anywhere on earth and, in his own estimation, one of his most important and ambitious projects.

Initial planning began in 1938 after the school's president, Dr. Ludd Spivey, made a compelling case to Wright that he should design and build a unique campus to bring the college international acclaim. Wright agreed, realizing that it would be an opportunity to test out his "Broadacre City" idea of urban planning.

The first 12 buildings were completed by 1958. The project paused for a time following Wright's death in 1959, but it resumed with completion of the last six structures. The buildings were together designated a National Historic Landmark in 2012 and ranked eighth in the AIA's list *Florida Architecture: 100 Years. 100 Places.*

The buildings include two chapels (the Danforth and the Pfeiffer), the Polk Science Building (which features the only Wright-designed planetarium), the circular Water Dome fountain,

---

In 2014 Central Florida became home to another visually stunning, award-winning architectural masterpiece: the Florida Polytechnic University Innovation, Science and Technology (IST) Building designed by Dr. Santiago Calatrava.

More than a dozen Frank Lloyd Wright structures make Florida Southern College an architect's dream campus.

a Usonian house and visitor center, a circular library, and the Esplanade, which connects the various buildings with a blend of Prairie and Mayan Revival styles completed with geometric representations and references to orange trees.

The choice of construction materials led to problems over the years, as their porous nature made them prone to leaks and water damage. Thankfully the buildings have been restored through grants and generous donations.

What: Florida Southern College

Where: 111 Lake Hollingsworth Dr., Lakeland

Cost: Self-guided tour, free; tour of the Usonian house, $10; other guided tours range from the $25 After Dark Tour to the $65 Behind the Scenes Tour

Pro Tip: If you're over six feet tall, be prepared to duck when passing through walkways and doors—otherwise the architecture may leave the wrong kind of impression on you.

FLOTSAM AND JETSAM

If an artistically inclined mermaid pirate opened a curio shop, what would it look like?

Did you dream of growing up aboard a cargo ship packed with art, antiques, and briny booty? Do old steamer trunks and treasure chests excite you? Does the phrase "maritime marvels and curiosities" fill you with boundless joy? If you answered yes to any of these questions, you're going to love the Sea Hagg.

A fixture in the town of Cortez since 1998, the Sea Hagg defies any simple description. It might be best to think of it as a hybrid nautical antique store, *Wunderkammer*, and salvage garden/outsider artwork installation.

Owner Jan Holman estimates that the contents of her store amount to over a million dollars' worth of plaster mermaids, pirate sculptures, mirrors, lanterns, anchors, coins, buoys, shells, and whatever else might be tucked away on the shelves. One assumes that her valuation encompasses the seashell-coated African fertility chair, the 16-foot sawfish bill, the "Grandmother Willow" from the Disney film *Pocahontas*, and the skull-adorned shrimp boat *Deanna Belle*. Any or all of this can be yours for a price. It's not clear if the painted "mermaid mobile" usually parked out front is also for sale, but there's no harm in asking.

Cortez Village itself is also a rare and priceless find—as one of the few remaining fishing villages in Florida, its residents have proudly and fiercely preserved it from the overdevelopment that is all too common along the Gulf Coast.

The assortment of goods at the Sea Hagg seems to change almost as often as the tides.

CASTING A WIDE NET

What: Sea Hagg

Where: 21649 US Hwy. 19 N., Clearwater

Cost: Free to browse

Pro Tip: According to its website, Sea Hagg will not allow you to gladly pay them Tuesday for a hamburger today. Or any day for that matter, as they do not sell hamburgers.

If you're in the market for something more interesting than the tchotchkes that fill countless beach tourist shops, this is your place. Who knows, maybe you'll find a wish-granting monkey's paw or an adorable little mogwai for the kids.

Beyond just shopping, the Sea Hagg also serves as a venue for a variety of events, including book signings, fishing festivals, and, naturally, a pirate treasure show.

FORGET NOT THY BEACH TOWEL, EZEKIEL

Do the Amish and Mennonites ever go on beach vacations?

Raising barns, farming, praying, managing livestock, cooking, churning butter, hand-washing clothing—the life of Amish and Mennonite men and women entails a lot of hard work, made all the more difficult in cold, northern climates. And sometimes everyone is entitled to a little more than just one day of rest each week. Well, hang on to your beards and bonnets and hop on the bus to Pinecraft, a beach neighborhood on the edge of Sarasota that caters to those with very specific requirements.

In the 1920s the Sarasota National Tourist Camp changed its name to Pinecraft, thereby encompassing all of the 466 campsites in the vicinity. In 1946 Pinecraft merged with another tourist camp, Homecroft, and that same year the Mennonite Tourist Church was established. By the 1950s there was a steady stream of seasonal visitors from Amish and Mennonite camps as far away as Ohio, Indiana, and Pennsylvania.

Today, the town has roughly 3,000 residents inhabiting small bungalows with plenty of non-technological activities to partake in. You'll see humbly dressed families riding tricycles along streets with names like Yoder, Kauffman, Schrock, and Fry on their

---

The Amish and Mennonites share many of the same core beliefs, but the Amish more strictly forbid any modern technology, whereas the Mennonites make some allowances for it and participate in missionary work abroad.

148

On the walls outside of Yoder's market is a mural with scenes from Amish and Mennonite life.

SUNSCREEN, AMOS!

What: Pinecraft

Where: On the edge of Sarasota, about an hour south of Tampa

Cost: Free

Pro Tip: Be respectful: pointing, gawking, and especially taking photos of the Amish and Mennonite vacationers are frowned upon.

way to and from the beach, churches, shuffleboard courts, Der Dutchman for a meal, or Big Olaf for ice cream. Inside the only Amish-run post office in the United States you can pick up your parcels, along with some practical wisdom from the handwritten notes tacked to the wall. You can also find a large mural outside of Yoder's Market that depicts Amish and Mennonites hard at work in their more traditional activities.

A DOUBLEHEADER IN SEMINOLE HEIGHTS

Why is one Tampa neighborhood fixated on two-headed alligators?

Looking out your window as you drive along North Nebraska Avenue, you might glimpse a two-headed alligator painted on the wall of a restaurant. Then, across the street you might catch something shimmering in the sunlight, which turns out to be the mosaic statue of a two-headed alligator (named "Bite or Smite") in front of Southern Brewing & Winemaking. Or perhaps you stop in to Ella's Americana Folk Art Cafe for a refreshing jalapeño-infused margarita, only to find yourself staring into the dual sets of dead reptilian eyes belonging to a stuffed two-headed alligator standing up on its hind legs from a shelf by the door.

Noticing a pattern?

Seminole Heights' adoption of the two-headed gator mascot dates back at least to 1911, when a local developer used the image in its marketing materials. Since then there have been occasional reports of such mutants, the most recent of which occurred in 2014 when local resident Justin Arnold snapped a picture which ran in the *Tampa Bay Times*. Despite debate over the authenticity of the picture, it is that very same gator that Ella's claims to have on display today.

Neither reptiles nor Seminole Heights has cornered the market on polycephaly—if you prefer doubleheaders of the mammalian variety, check to see if "Half 'n' Half the Two-Headed Calf" is on display at the St. Petersburg Museum of History.

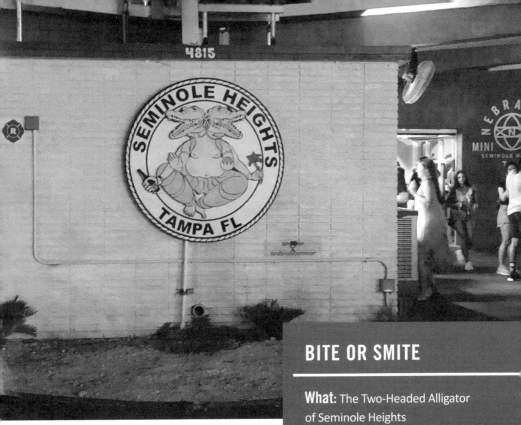

Nebraska Mini Mart is one of several places in Seminole Heights where you'll find the image of a two-headed alligator.

BITE OR SMITE

What: The Two-Headed Alligator of Seminole Heights

Where: Ella's Americana Folk Art Cafe and other locations

Cost: Free to view

Pro Tip: In addition to having the alleged actual alligator on display, Ella's also has a trove of outsider art and a "Wall of Elvis" worth seeing, not to mention stellar food and beverages.

Polycephaly, the condition of having more than one head, while rare, does occur in nature and seems to have a preference for reptiles. One potential reason for this may be that reptiles tend to have more offspring, so simply playing the genetic numbers game means a greater change of mutation. Another possibility is that eggs laid rather than carried in the body have greater exposure to environmental factors.

Ultimately, however infrequent the condition may be, you can always find a two-headed gator in Seminole Heights.

TAMPA'S RESTAURANT ROYALTY

What's the recipe for success at the oldest restaurant in Florida?

Restaurants seem to come and go almost faster than you can place your order, but in Tampa one family-owned restaurant has been serving up Spanish food and culture for more than a century. Founded in 1905 as a 60-seat corner café by Cuban immigrant Casimiro Hernandez Sr., Columbia has become an Ybor City institution recognized as the oldest continually operating restaurant in Florida and both the oldest and largest Spanish restaurant in the United States.

You might think that 15 dining rooms with 1,700 seats occupying 52,000 square feet—a full city block—would be hard to fill, but you'll still want to make your reservations well ahead of time, especially if you want a table with a view of the live flamenco dance shows offered Monday through Saturday. Each of the dining rooms features Moorish-style architecture and ornaments that enhance the sense of dining like Spanish nobility. The menu includes variations on traditional staples such as gazpacho, ropa vieja, and flan, as well as the family's own selection of wines.

Columbia remains a family business run today by the fourth and fifth generations of the Hernandez family. Casimiro Sr. passed away in 1929, leaving control of the restaurant to Casimiro Jr., who added dancing in the first air-conditioned dining room in Tampa, the

---

In 2010 Columbia became one of only 50 restaurants in the United States honored as an All-American Icon by *Nation's Restaurant News*.

The artwork, architecture, and ornaments such as coats of arms and fountains give Columbia an old world ambience.

Don Quixote Room. Ownership passed to Casimiro Jr.'s daughter Adela and her husband Cesar Gonzmart, who began opening other locations. Following Cesar's death in 1992, his sons Casey and Richard took over and now run the business with their own children. They also own the burger chain Goody Goody and farm-to-fork restaurant and brewery Ulele.

THE FAMILY BUSINESS

What: Columbia Restaurant

Where: There are seven locations, but the original is in Ybor City at 2117 E. Seventh Ave., Tampa.

Cost: Variable, but $120 is probably a good median estimate for dinner and drinks for two.

Pro Tip: You can't go wrong with anything on the menu at Columbia, but if you want something unique, try the signature 1905 salad, which is made tableside.

USE WELL THESE FEW BUT EVER FLEETING HOURS

Does Tampa Bay have any remarkable timepieces?

With so much to see and experience in Tampa Bay, it's easy to lose track of time. Perhaps that's why you'll find so many unusual clocks and timekeeping artworks throughout the area.

To start with, there's the sundial in the courtyard of the shopping, dining, and entertainment complex known, fittingly, as Sundial St. Pete. The sundial was designed by René Lagler and is ringed by a mosaic lagoon and six bronze dolphins. It rises to a height of roughly two stories, which, according to the plaque on its base, makes it the largest in the world, as certified in 2014 by the North American Sundial Society.

A second, less well-known but no less impressive temporal artwork can be found standing by the corner of Tampa Union Station. Titled *Tampa Centennial Keep*, this 28-foot-tall clock tower was designed by William C. Culbertson through the city's public artwork program and tells the station's history, which spans a century. Carved into the tower you'll find Henry B. Plant; a tribute to the station's first stationmaster, Harry Love; and images related to the three railroad companies that built the station, the Atlantic Coast Line, the Seaboard Air Line, and the Tampa Northern.

If you visit some of the restaurants on Anna Maria Island, you can also participate in the island's tradition of betting on the exact time of sunset.

The sundial in the center of the eponymously named Sundial St. Pete claims to be the largest in the world.

A third, more somber public timepiece can be found at Bayshore and Bay to Bay Boulevards in the form of a 9/11 memorial. The two towers of the World Trade Center are represented as outlines using aluminum. Inside one of these is a steel I-beam from the North Tower, which acts as a sundial. It measures not the time of day, but rather, on September 11 each year, the 102 minutes from when the north tower was initially struck by a plane to when it collapsed.

A TOWERING ENIGMA

Why is there a lighthouse along the Hillsborough River?

If you've driven on I-275 you've probably noticed the 214-foot-tall white tower along the river. It's rather hard to miss. But for being so visible, its history and function are less obvious—most assume it's either an oddly placed lighthouse or the remnants of a castle or military fort.

The real history of the tower is that it was built in 1927 by Grover Poole to supply water to an ill-fated resort spa and tourist attraction. The project was the brainchild of developer Josiah S. Richardson, who planned to expand his Sulphur Springs Hotel and Apartments (which also housed Mave's Arcade, the first shopping mall in Florida). Before Richardson could see his plan through, his property ended up underwater, literally, when the TECO dam collapsed and flooded the area in 1933.

For the next 38 years, the tower served as a private water

LOFTY AMBITIONS

What: Sulphur Springs Water Tower

Where: 6455–479 E. Bird St., Tampa

Cost: Free

Pro Tip: It's boarded up because it is not safe to enter or climb.

A boarded-up and slowly decaying tower inevitably becomes the subject of local lore about ancient Tocobaga curses, lost pirate treasure, and ghost stories—but historically, only investors have anything to fear from this site.

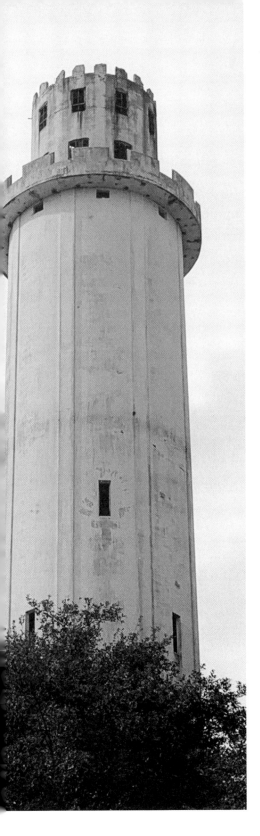

Sulphur Springs Tower is a well-known landmark with a not so well-known history.

company, piping artesian well water to local residents and businesses. In 1971 the company was forced out of business by the city to further its own water utility operation. For a brief period around 1951 a drive-in theater operated next to the tower, but an aircraft warning light was said to make watching movies difficult. Efforts to build high-end apartments and condos there fizzled out in the 1980s. In 2002 one of the big-box drugstores put a bid on the site, but public outcry killed the initiative. In 2005 it was acquired by the city as the central feature of River Tower Park.

Today the tower stands vacant like a silent sentinel out of time and place, waiting for a renewed purpose. Recently there have been efforts to restore and open to the public this historic tower that is far more loved than understood.

DEAD MEN TELL TALL TALES

Was Charlie Smith really 137 years old when he died?

Less than an hour east of Tampa is the town of Bartow, where one of the local residents is still telling his improbable origin story from beyond the grave. The tombstone of Charlie Smith proclaims him to be "America's Oldest Man," which is almost certainly a fabrication. But then Charlie was apparently never one to let facts get in the way of a great origin story.

Smith claimed to have been born in Liberia in 1842, kidnapped at the age of 12 and brought to the United States, where he was sold into slavery. From there he was bought by a Texas farmer named Charlie Smith, who treated the young boy as his own.

Upon Charlie Sr.'s death, the boy assumed his name, joined the Union army, and then traveled West, where his adventures become increasingly unlikely, from serving as a ranch hand and a professional gambler to falling in with the James Gang and chasing Billy the Kid as a bounty hunter, before ending up in a circus sideshow.

His story was captured in a 1978 episode of the television series Visions titled "Charlie Smith and the Fritter Tree," in which Smith narrates his tale to a nursing home orderly through a series of flashbacks.

In 1972, Charlie was invited to view the Apollo 17 launch at the Kennedy Space Center, but he remained skeptical that the rocket he saw was actually going to the moon.

CHARLIE SMITH
JULY 4, 1842
OCT. 5, 1979
AMERICA'S OLDEST MAN

Charlie Smith's tombstone serves as a reminder that you can't believe everything you read, even if it's carved stone.

FRITTER AWAY THE FACTS

What: The grave of Charlie Smith

Where: Wildwood Cemetery, 985 Square Lake Dr., Bartow

Cost: Free

Pro Tip: The tombstone is in row 28, second in from the wall.

While Smith's actual age remains unconfirmed, he most likely was a centenarian. A marriage certificate for Smith and Bell Van issued on January 8, 1910, lists his age as 35 and his place of birth as Georgia. There are also census documents listing a Mr. Smith as being 21 in the year 1900.

True or not, three years after his passing, the town purchased a tombstone for him in the local cemetery, along with his self-proclaimed title.

159

MOLLY THE MOLLUSK

Where can you see a real sea monster up close?

Since ancient times, the ocean has been a source of fascination, mystery, and sometimes terror. Just a cursory glance at old maps will reveal a menagerie of monsters, including sea dragons, hags, demons, and, let's not forget, the fabled kraken.

While many of these are fabrications, at least some have a basis in reality. For example, consider that last one, the humongous, ship-devouring kraken. Could it be that this creature was based on a rare sighting of a giant squid? For the answer to that, you'll want to head south from Tampa to the Mote Marine Laboratory & Aquarium, where you can judge for yourself.

Meet Molly the Mollusk, a 27-foot-long giant squid preserved in the Exploration Gallery. Molly was caught by a fishing trawler off the coast of New Zealand on March 15, 1999, and shipped that same

RELEASE THE KRAKEN!

What: Mote Marine Laboratory & Aquarium

Where: 1600 Ken Thompson Pkwy., Sarasota

Cost: Adults, $24; youths, $18

Pro Tip: The Mote actually consists of two different buildings on opposite sides of the parking lot—your ticket gets you into both.

Mote to the rescue: the stranding investigations program responds to more than 100 incidents involving dolphins and sea turtles each year, and, in the lab, researchers are cultivating over 13,000 colonies of threatened staghorn coral.

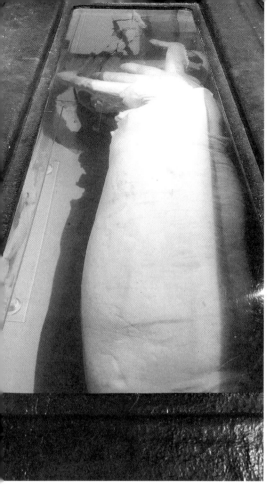

Molly has been a sea monster in residence at Mote for more than 20 years.

year to the Mote. While she sometimes travels the country posthumously as part of a Sea Monsters exhibit, she has recently returned home to Sarasota.

Given the rarity of encounters with colossal squid, Molly has been invaluable in filling in some of the gaps in researchers' knowledge. What we do know is that a length of up to 46 feet and a weight of as much as 1,650 pounds makes these deep-sea denizens the largest known invertebrates on Earth. They also have the largest eyes in the animal kingdom (up to 11 inches in diameter).

Molly alone makes the Mote worth a visit, but she's just one of many fascinating creatures that you'll find there, including jellyfish, sharks, reef animals, rays, manatees, otters, and others. And if you feel the need to take flight from the inhabitants of the depths, you can visit the Save Our Seabirds sanctuary and learning center across the parking lot.

CASTLE IN THE SWAMP

Can the phrase "a man's home is his castle" be taken too literally?

When outsider artist, sculptor, and author Howard Solomon moved to Florida with his family in 1972, his neighbors found him both peculiar and fascinating. The peculiar part didn't bother him—as a child he'd been branded as mentally deficient by conventional educators. But as an artist (called by some "the da Vinci of Debris"), his ability to see beyond the material at hand and instead envision what might be was a gift rather than a handicap. While others saw Ona as nearly worthless swampland, Solomon saw the land upon which he would create his home and studio, which he did, by hand. In 1974, when a local newspaper went out of business, while others saw useless stacks of aluminum printing plates, Solomon recognized it as the metal from which he would construct his own gleaming metal fortress. Which he did, again, by hand.

THE WISDOM OF SOLOMON

What: Solomon's Castle

Where: 4533 Solomon Rd., Ona

Cost: 45-minute castle tour, $18; the encore, $10; both tours, $24 (all prices for adults)

Pro Tip: The mosquitos can get very aggressive—be sure to pack some bug repellant.

Would it surprise you to learn that there are at least two other DIY castles in Florida? The most famous of these is Ed Leedskalnin's Coral Castle in Homestead, and a more recent development is Castle Otttis (yes, with three t's) in St. Augustine.

Top: Howard Solomon's most famous work of art was also his residence.
Right: He later added the boat in the moat.

The completed three-story castle spanned roughly 10,000 square feet, with a courtyard and more than 80 interpretive stained-glass windows and found object artworks fashioned from coat hangers, car parts, beer cans, and anything else Solomon could find. Not surprisingly, Solomon's Castle became a quirky roadside attraction, which he was only too happy to share with visitors.

But why stop with just a castle? Solomon next constructred the Boat-in-the-Moat—a 60-foot-long Spanish galleon with three masts that doubles as a restaurant)—and the Lily Life House, a lighthouse connected to a pavilion.

Although Solomon passed away in 2016, his family continues to operate the attraction. Solomon, known as much for his wit as for his artwork, lives on in the pun-laden tour which has remained true to the script he devised.

FROM HARD LUCK TO HARD ROCK

How did the discovery of a Seminole burial ground in Tampa help deal the tribe a winning hand?

That the Seminole people were never officially defeated by the United States is a point of pride for members of that tribe in what is an otherwise dark story of conflict, cruelty, forced removal, and disenfranchisement.

Franklin Delano Roosevelt sought to address this in 1934 through the Indian Reorganization Act, which granted tribes like the Seminoles certain tax exemptions and the right to self-governance. Little did anyone realize that these seeds would blossom into a multibillion-dollar casino and gaming empire.

Under Chief Jim Billie in 1979, the Seminoles became the first tribe in North America to open up high-stakes bingo on their land—a move as controversial as the man who made it. But it quickly transformed the tribe's meager income from selling tribal souvenirs to tourists to raking in millions of dollars from gaming. A landmark 1981 case further cemented the Seminoles' gaming rights in Florida.

Around that same time, parking garage developers in Tampa discovered the remains of 144 Native Americans, which led the Seminole tribe to deem the land a sacred burial site. The city

---

It wouldn't be a Hard Rock without an impressive collection of memorabilia, including a Jimi Hendrix pastel stage scarf, a white corset dress worn by Stevie Nicks, and just recently acquired: the iconic gold piano that belonged to Elvis.

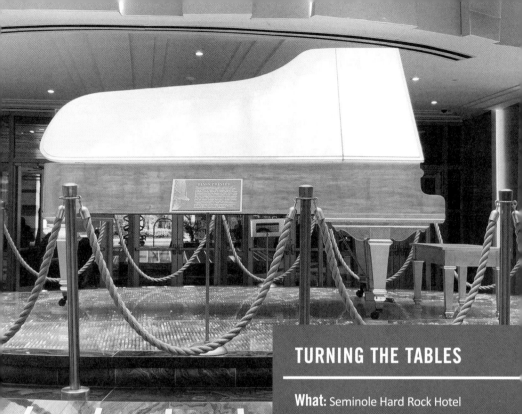

The golden piano is not Tampa's only connection to Elvis Presley—he also spent time in the area during the filming of "Follow That Dream."

acquired eight and a half acres of land at the intersection of I-4 and Orient Road for a land swap. From their new Tampa land, the tribe began selling tax-free cigarettes and opened a bingo hall, which was developed into the Seminole Hard Rock Hotel & Casino in 2004. Operating 24 hours a day, it's now one of the largest casinos in the world, with 245,000 square feet of gaming space that includes 5,000 slot machines, 179 table games, and 46 poker tables. It continues to accrue an impressive list of awards as a top-rated hotel and one of the largest employers in the Tampa Bay area.

STEAM ENGINES OF WAR

What's French for steampunk?

Throughout the Sunshine State you'll find tributes to our deep and enduring love affair with the automobile, from the Don Garlits Museum of Drag Racing to the Sarasota Classic Car Museum and racetracks in Daytona and Sebring. While all these collections showcase unique and impressive feats of engineering, few show the full history and development of motorized vehicles like the Tampa Bay Automobile Museum.

Each vehicle was selected for its unique contribution to the evolution of automobiles, such as pioneering front-wheel drive and rear engine cars. You'll find here some exceedingly rare vehicles from automotive engineering pioneers like Tracta, Citroën, Voisin, Tatra, Alvis, DeLorean, and others. Yes, the museum has many gems, but its one true crown jewel is the Fardier de Cugnot.

It was completed in 2010 as engineers from Polypack and TBAUTO collaborated to bring to life the only known fully functioning, replica of the world's first self-propelled vehicle.

The original Fardier de Cugnot was constructed in 1770 by Nicolas-Joseph Cugnot in order to transport heavy military equipment. It has resided at le Conservatoire national des arts et métiers in Paris since 1801. The Tampa Bay version was designed to be faithful in every way to the original, from the wooden frame

---

If you're looking for another unique automotive experience in Tampa Bay, in mid-March each year you can catch the Firestone Grand Prix of St. Petersburg, which signals the opening of IndyCar racing season.

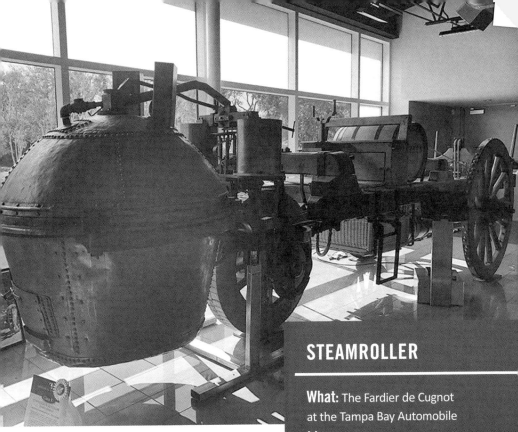

The Fardier de Cugnot, a marvel of engineering, more closely resembles a steam-belching catapult on wheels than a modern automobile.

STEAMROLLER

What: The Fardier de Cugnot at the Tampa Bay Automobile Museum

Where: 3301 Gateway Centre Blvd., Pinellas Park

Cost: Adults, $8; seniors, $6; youths, $5; children under the age of 12, free

Pro Tip: The museum is closed on Tuesdays and holidays.

to the bolts of the monstrous, spherical engine, which was the first of its kind to drive a piston in a cylinder using high-pressure steam.

Cugnot's design proved his machine a success by using it to pull a five-ton artillery cannon. This was not only a relief to the French military, but it ushered in the age of automobiles, reshaping the world in ways that Cugnot almost certainly never imagined.

SMALL WONDER

What is the smallest park in Florida?

You won't find much snow in Florida, and you won't find much Florida in Snow Park. Occupying the thin triangular sliver of land across the street from the University of Tampa where West Grand Central Avenue branches off from West Kennedy Boulevard, Snow Park spans just 150 square feet, with 13 oak trees and a small monument and fountain dedicated to Major Henry E. Snow.

At one time, Snow Park was recognized by both Ripley's Believe It or Not! and the *Guinness Book of World Records* as being the world's smallest park, but a number of micro parks have eclipsed it since then.

Don't let the size of the park fool you into thinking it's a commentary on the impact of the man to whom it was dedicated in 1921. Snow, originally from Harwichport, MA, was a father of four and, according to the *Tampa Bay Times*, one of the city's "best known and best loved citizens."

Snow served on the city's Board of Public Works in 1910 and

LET IT SNOW

What: Snow Park

Where: W. Kennedy Blvd. & W. Grand Central Ave., Tampa

Cost: Free

Pro Tip: It's on the same block as the Oxford Exchange, which is also worth a visit.

Florida is big on its miniature achievements—you can find the smallest post office in the United States in Ochopee, the world's smallest police station in Carrabelle, and the nation's narrowest street (Treasury Street) in St. Augustine.

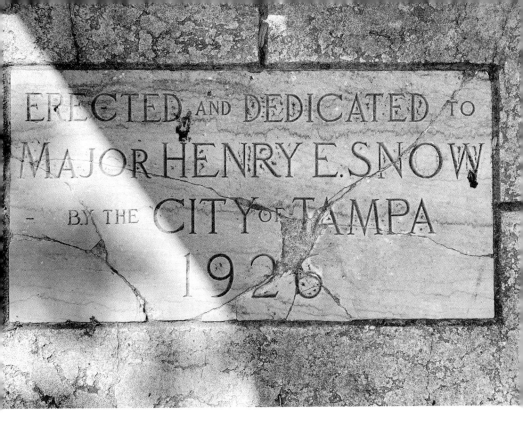

Snow Park lost its title as the smallest park in the nation to Mill's End Park in Portland, OR, which is just 452 square inches.

was reelected to serve three consecutive terms. He also served as a member of the city's first commission. City Hall, the Lafayette Street Bridge, the sewer system, the library, and a fire station were all constructed during his years in public service. He was also a Grand Marshal of the annual Gasparilla Parade, one of the founders of the South Florida Fair Association, and a supporter of both the Salvation Army and the Children's Home.

A marble monument was set at the foot of the covered fountain (which has since lost its roof) in 1926 following Snow's death.

PLAY IT AGAIN

Where can you join a pinball league?

Once upon a time, if you wanted to play video games with your friends, you had to visit an arcade. These dimly lit digital dens were sensory playgrounds with flashing multicolored lights, beeps and blips blaring from the rows of pinball machines, and video game kiosks like *Joust*, *Pac-Man*, *Spy Hunter*, and *Donkey Kong*, to name just a few. These games required quarters or tokens, and a skilled player could make a pocketful of change last for hours.

Today it seems that the 1980s are back in a big way, from books and movies like *Ready Player One* to the hit Netflix series *Stranger Things*. But you can't truly appreciate that decade without video game and pinball arcades—a challenge that the Replay Museum has gladly undertaken.

With over 125 working machines, the Replay Museum is the largest in central Florida. A display atop each pinball machine lets you see the artist, designer, company, number produced, and year it was released, thereby allowing you to play your way through entertainment history. Games here span the full evolution of pinball, from electromechanical to the numeric, alphanumeric, dot matrix display (DMD), and the current LCD machines. The hands-on collection includes popular titles like *Theater of Magic*; rarities like *Total Annihilation*, which allows for collaborative pinball play; a working 1968 Paul Bunyan pinball machine; and a massive, one-of-a-kind, custom-built Tron arcade game—what they refer to as their

Keep the nostalgia flowing with a visit to Bear Haven Land Company Vintage Toys, conveniently located next door.

The Replay Museum's collection lets you play your way through more than 50 years of pinball history.

"Jumbo Tron"—created at Tampa Hackerspace.

The museum also hosts tournaments for the International Flipper Pinball Association (IFPA) and the ladies league, Belles and Chimes, which is a welcome change for the historically male-dominated pastime.

PINHEAD PARADISE

What: Replay Museum

Where: 119 E. Tarpon Ave., Tarpon Springs

Cost: Daily admittance, which includes unlimited play, is adults, $14; children ages 7–12, $8; children age 6 and younger, free

Pro Tip: Fridays and Saturdays from 8–11 p.m. Replay has special late night/date night pricing: two for $22. The museum also buys, sells, and repairs vintage games.

JUICED

Has the citrus industry ever produced any unusual attractions around the Tampa Bay area?

If necessity is the mother of invention, what if Old Man Winter was the father? You'll find the answer to that question, along with a great many other questions you never realized you had, at Boyett's Grove and Citrus Attraction in Brooksville.

During the winter of 1962, exactly five years to the day from the previous freeze, temperatures in Tampa fell to as low as 18 degrees Fahrenheit (that's almost negative eight Celsius), which damaged citrus fruits and vegetables. Like many citrus farmers, Kathy and Jim Oleson were caught off guard and had to quickly come up with another way to generate revenue to keep their business afloat.

They decided to transform their grove and stand into an old-fashioned, 1950s-era roadside attraction following the formula of St. Pete's Sunken Gardens and Silver Springs State Park. They opened a wildlife park with horses, goats, emus, zebras, and, of course, alligators. To this they added a souvenir gift shop. And an ice cream parlor. And nature paths. And a pirate gallery with a large aquarium. And a tropical bird aviary featuring colorful (and loud) macaws. And a miniature golf course with a stagecoach and other handmade sets. And a monkey beach. And a prehistoric-themed cave featuring animated dinosaurs. And, more recently, a 3-D art

---

The Olesons weren't the only ones to have the idea of transforming their citrus grove into something more unusual. At the Showcase of Citrus in Clermont you can pick oranges and go on a swamp safari ... in the world's largest monster truck.

Born of necessity, Boyett's Grove and Citrus Attraction has become a continually evolving maze of novelty gifts and entertainment.

HOMEGROWN

What: Boyett's Grove and Citrus Attraction

Where: 4355 Spring Lake Hwy., Brooksville

Cost: The main gift shop is free; some sections and activities have their own costs.

Pro Tip: The interior is ever evolving, so don't expect things to be in the same place as the last time you visited.

gallery and a *Predator and Prey* taxidermy display, and a lifelike Elvis strumming a guitar because, hey, why not?

From October through June you can still watch citrus being cleaned, processed, and packaged, but with everything else now going on at the attraction, the fruit almost seems like an afterthought.

BRIDGE OVER TROUBLED WATER

What happened to the original Sunshine Skyway Bridge?

Rising 430 feet into the air, the 4.14-mile long Bob Graham Sunshine Skyway Bridge connecting St. Petersburg in Pinellas County and Terra Ceia in Manatee County is the steepest and second-longest bridge in Florida. It is also the second bridge with that name and location. Even drivers who aren't terrified of its rollercoaster-like ascent and descent might take greater care upon learning the tragic history of the bridge and surrounding waters.

At 7:33 a.m. on May 9, 1980, a sudden squall sent the Liberian phosphate freighter MV *Summit Venture* crashing through the dense fog and into a support column, causing 1,400 feet of the highway bridge to collapse. A total of seven vehicles, including a Greyhound bus, plunged into the bay below, killing 35 people. Miraculously, one Wesley MacIntire survived when his truck first hit the deck of the boat before the water, buying him a few extra seconds to escape. The pilot of the *Summit Venture*, John E. Lerro, was cleared of wrongdoing following investigations by both the Coast Guard and a state grand jury, but he retired shortly thereafter due to health reasons.

The Sunshine Skyway Bridge actually spans three different counties: Manatee County on one end, Pinellas County on the other, and Hillsboro County, which claims the shipping lane that runs below the bridge.

The anchor of the USCGC Blackthorn *is one of the memorials you can visit at the Sunshine Skyway Bridge north rest area.*

Sadly, the Skyway Bridge disaster was neither the only nor the first deadly maritime mishap of 1980. Earlier, on January 28th of that year, the US Coast Guard Cutter *Blackthorn* capsized after colliding with the tanker SS *Capricorn* in the waters near the bridge. Twenty-three crew members perished, making it the deadliest peacetime Coast Guard wreck in modern history.

You can pay your respects to the victims of both tragedies at Blackthorn Memorial Park in St. Petersburg.

THE LOST CEMETERIES OF HILLSBOROUGH

How does a city lose track of a half-dozen cemeteries?

With indigenous people having lived in Florida for 12,000 years or more, it's not all that uncommon to discover bodies beneath commercial or residential buildings. Every once in a while, though, those human remains are far greater in number and much more recent than you might expect. Such is the case with the recently rediscovered Zion Cemetery, one of Tampa's first black cemeteries, which was hidden under the Robles Park neighborhood in Tampa Heights for nearly 70 years.

A cemetery may not sound like the sort of thing that's easy to lose, but it continues to happen throughout Florida, especially to older African American cemeteries that were not as well preserved and were built over by eager developers. If not for a cemetery historian who contacted the *Tampa Bay Times* in the fall of 2018 for assistance in tracking down Zion Cemetery, the burial ground would likely have remained lost beneath public housing from the 1950s.

It took time and dedication, walking all of Memorial Cemetery, the city's other black cemetery from the time, and combing through as many as 30,000 death certificates and records, but journalist Paul Guzzo was able to determine the approximate location of

---

Even more recently than the discovery of Zion Cemetery, roughly 145 coffins were found under Tampa's King High School in November 2019, possibly part of Ridgewood Cemetary. Local historians expect still more to be found in the near future.

Zion Cemetery was hidden for nearly 70 years beneath public housing.

MATTERS OF GRAVE CONCERN

What: The Lost Cemeteries of Hillsborough

Where: If we knew that, they wouldn't be lost.

Cost: Free

Pro Tip: If you visit, be very sensitive—it's a painful situation for relatives of the deceased, as well as for residents who may have to relocate.

Zion. Following this, with the help of ground-penetrating radar, archeologists from USF have found what they believe to be more than 130 gravesites under part of the Robles Park apartment complex.

The Tampa Housing Authority has relocated 96 residents from five buildings while researchers attempt to locate and notify all next of kin. State Senator Janet Cruz has filed a bill to provide funds for both a memorial and a task force to research and locate other lost cemeteries in Hillsborough. These efforts will hopefully spare Tampa residents from similar surprises in the future.

AN ISLAND IN THE SUN

Where can you find a hidden beach, a nature preserve, and a ruined military fort all in the same place?

If you feel the need to get out of the city and find a secluded spot to recharge and reconnect with nature, Tampa Bay has numerous parks and trails. But among the lesser known local getaways, Egmont Key is special for a number of reasons.

For one thing, it's accessible only by boat. If you don't have one of your own, not to worry; you can catch a ferry from Fort De Soto. Once there, you'll have 440 acres to roam. Since it is both a state park and wildlife refuge, most days you'll probably encounter more gopher tortoises and bottle nose dolphins than other human beings. In addition to hiking the trails and beaches, there's excellent shelling, fishing, and snorkeling.

And there's a surprising amount of history to the island as well. Seminoles captured during the Seminole Wars were interred there while awaiting relocation to Arkansas and Oklahoma. Among such Seminoles was Polly Parker (Madeloyee) who, along with a dozen others on May 4, 1858, escaped when their boat stopped briefly at St. Marks to take on wood for its boilers. They then made their way by foot roughly 400 miles back to their home near Lake Okeechobee. When news of her escape spread, it elevated Parker to folk hero status.

A similarly hidden gem in terms of unsullied and seldom-crowded beaches is Caladesi Island, accessible via ferry from Honeymoon Island State Park.

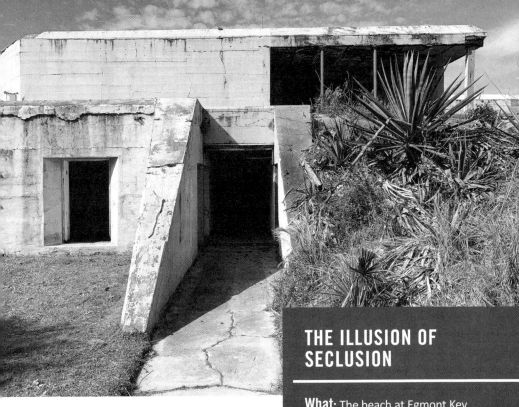

The ruins of Fort Dade are an urban explorer's dream come true.

THE ILLUSION OF SECLUSION

What: The beach at Egmont Key

Where: Egmont Key State Park

Cost: If you plan to climb among the ruins, watch out for the barnacles. They're sharper than you might realize.

Pro Tip: There are no shops, restaurants, or running water on Egmont Key, so bring everything you need with you.

The same year that Parker escaped, the tallest man-made structure on the island was erected. The lighthouse still stands today, reaching a height of 87 feet. Fort Dade was built on the island during the Spanish–American War, along with various administrative offices and housing. Today the ruins of the fort and the surrounding ghost town make a unique setting for exploration.

THERE CAN BE ONLY ONE

Is that . . . bagpipe music?

You could make a compelling case that Dunedin does strange in all the best ways. As the fifth-largest city in Pinellas County, it is notable for its open waterfront, its absence of big corporate franchise stores and restaurants, its demonstrated commitment to local arts, and its Scottish heritage. "Celtic" isn't a word that comes naturally to mind when describing Florida's beaches, but it was two Scottish merchants, J. O. Douglas and James Somerville, who gave the town its name, which comes from the Gaelic name for "Edinburgh," in 1882. Since then, the town has proudly displayed its Celtic roots while maintaining close ties to its sister cities Stirling, Scotland, and Summerside, Prince Edward Island, Canada.

Keeping that heritage and history front and center every year for more than half a century, Dunedin has hosted the Highland Games & Festival, in which various clans register and compete in a variety of activities. The event begins with the arrival of the Chieftain at the head of a pipe marching band and parade down Main Street, with kilts and colorful plaid tartans on full display.

Following this are the various competitions, including solo piping, pipe bands, highland dancing, a Highland Train 5K run, and other feats of athleticism.

The City of Dunedin Pipe Band is top ranked and recognized internationally. In 2018 the band took home the title of World Champions—Grade 2 from the World Pipe Band Championship in Glasgow, Scotland.

If you miss the Highland Games, you can still enjoy a piper on the pier most Friday evenings.

Unlike the popular film *Highlander*, there is no quickening and the winners are granted immortality only insofar as their achievements are recorded for all time. Thankfully, this also means that all the contestants who don't come in first place still get to keep their heads and compete again the following year.

IF YE LIKE THE NUT, CRACK IT

What: The Highland Games

Where: 1920 Pinehurst Rd., Dunedin

Cost: Early Bird general admission, $15; VIP ticket, including all-day food and drink, $100

Pro Tip: If you want to find out more about Dunedin's unique history, check out the Dunedin History Museum.

TINY TERRORS

Why do the words "Mini Lights" strike fear into the hearts of some longtime residents of St. Pete?

For decades an urban legend has been keeping the residents of St. Petersburg's Roser Park neighborhood off the streets and out of the parks at night. There are plenty of variations on the tale, but most involve an old woman who lived with two diminutive minions (possibly midget circus performers). The city confiscated her land to create a park, of which, predictably, she did not approve. Every night she would exact her revenge by sending forth her two assistants to terrorize anyone they found. These supernatural helpers are now said to appear as either little orbs of light or small green people summoned by uttering the phrase "Mini Lights come out tonight" three times (a la Beetlejuice or Bloody Mary).

In some versions of the story, the woman's name was Minnie (hence "Minnie Lights"). Yet other variants of the story require circling her home three times, which of course entails knowing the location of her former abode—a topic on which there is virtually no agreement.

The story may have become entwined with another local legend about Merry Lights, a troll said to live under the Booker Creek Bridge that can be drawn out by thrice repeating its name.

As for trolls living under bridges, this idea likely originated in Scandinavian folklore and made its way to the English-speaking world via stories such as "Three Billy Goats Gruff."

Many of the Mini Lights sightings are concentrated around Booker Creek.

LITTLE GREEN MEANIES

What: Mini Lights (also sometimes known as Midget Lights or Merry Lights)

Where: Roser Park neighborhood along Booker Creek in St. Petersburg

Cost: None, except possibly your life

Pro Tip: Mini lights aside, stumbling around parks and creeks late at night can be dangerous—take proper precautions.

In 2017 the creative trio known as the Vitale Bros., launched a project to produce a Blair Witch-style film about the Mini Lights. Their adaptation traces the origin of the story to a more tragic yet believable scenario in which alligator hunters would raid local homes of African American families, abduct the children, tie them up, and leave them by riverbanks as bait. The flickering of the hunters' lanterns as they approached might be the origin of the mini lights coming to claim their victims.

CREATIVE TRANSFORMATION

How did artwork enable Marietta Lee to triumph over tragedy?

The word "whimsical" has a few different definitions, but for our purposes, let's look at the one that explains it as "light, fanciful, and subject to unpredictable change." Why that particular definition? Because it applies perfectly not only to the contents of the Marietta Museum of Art & Whimsy, but also to its origin.

Long before Marietta Lee established her museum and gallery full of brightly colored and polka-dotted artworks and sculptures in Sarasota, she was pursuing a very different line of work. Her education and training took place in Kentucky, where she became an RN, EMT, and paramedic, always ready to deliver lifesaving medical care. But when she was called to the scene of an airplane crash with no survivors, what she saw was too much to process. She began sketching the crash from memory as a means of trying to make sense of what she had witnessed, and in doing so underwent what certainly qualifies as an unpredictable change: she realized that art was her passion and calling.

She went back to.school, earning a Bachelor of Fine Arts from the Ringling College of Art and Design. In 2006, after serving as a fulltime caregiver for her parents, she was able to pursue her dream of opening a museum, which found a permanent home in Sarasota two years later.

Art therapy has been around since the 1940s, and Margaret Naumburg is widely regarded as its founder.

A sound-activated kinetic artwork hangs from the ceiling at the Marietta Museum of Art & Whimsy.

LAUGHTER IS THE BEST MEDICINE

What: Marietta Museum of Art & Whimsy

Where: 2121 N. Tamiami Tr., Sarasota

Cost: $5 suggested donation (cash only)

Pro Tip: Open seasonally from 1–4 p.m. Thursdays, Fridays, and Saturdays.

Today the roster of artists and artworks is ever changing, but you can usually find flying pink pigs in the garden, a kinetic sculpture suspended from the ceiling (it changes color in response to sound), the mosaic Lee Family Arch, and hundreds of other light and fanciful creations.

FOR WHOM THE BELLS TOLL

Where can you hear music made by the largest type of instrument in the world?

Rising from the top of Iron Mountain in Lake Wales, surrounded by a bird sanctuary and contemplative garden designed by Frederick Law Olmsted Jr., is a stunningly beautiful, 205-foot-tall "singing tower" that looks like it belongs more in Tolkien's Middle Earth than in Central Florida.

Edward Bok emigrated from the Netherlands to the United States at the age of six and became a successful publisher, the editor of *Ladies' Home Journal*, and a Pulitzer Prize-winning author. He retired in 1919, although he continued various humanitarian endeavors, and decided in 1921 to preserve the hilltop near his winter home as a bird sanctuary and place of peace and serenity. Work on the tower began in 1924 and took five years to complete. President Calvin Coolidge dedicated Bok Tower Gardens on February 1, 1929. The full scope of his gift includes not only the tower and a 250-acre garden, but also the Pine Ridge Trail, Pinewood Estate, and a visitor center.

The tower houses a 60-bell carillon—the largest bell weighs 11.7 tons—that plays twice a day at 1 p.m. and 3 p.m. Ringed with a reflective moat and composed of pink coquina, brick, marble,

A popular place to stop on the way to Bok Tower Gardens is Spook Hill, where people put their cars in neutral and watch as their automobiles seem to defy gravity and roll uphill thanks to an optical illusion.

The north side of the tower contains the only entrance, through brass doors depicting the book of Genesis.

THE SINGING TOWER

What: Bok Tower Gardens

Where: 1151 Tower Blvd., Lake Wales

Cost: Garden admission is adults, $15; children ages 5–12, $5; children ages 4 and under, free; dogs, $5

Pro Tip: Bok Tower Gardens frequently has special events throughout the year—check the calendar on its website.

and structural steel, the tower is the vision of Milton B. Medary. It has been described as a fusion of neo-Gothic and art deco styles, resulting in long, straight lines adorned with elaborate marble sculptures, colored tiles, and iron gates and railings.

When he died in 1930, Bok was interred at the base of the tower—a small but permanent place within his gift to the American people.

187

MORE THAN JUST A WHIM

Can you live and work inside a giant mosaic artwork?

Whimzeyland, or the "Bowling Ball House," as it's sometimes known, is impossible to miss. Artists and childhood sweethearts Todd Ramquist and Kiaralinda have turned their home and studio—a perpetual work in progress more than 30 years in the making—into a mosaic and recycled art paradise. Prismatic pathways wind around the outside of the house, past playful and vibrant glass and metal works.

And bowling balls. Lots of bowling balls. More than 800 of them at last count, arranged along flower beds and assembled into pyramids and other shapes. The duo began acquiring these unusual creative components when they happened upon a flea market that was offering "ten free bowling balls per person." With the help of their friends, they acquired 60 balls, and from there the collection kept rolling as other creative and like-minded locals started decorating and donating more.

The couple obtained and added to the property a gazebo from the old Kapok Tree Inn. But the creativity was not to be contained there, as it continued to spread across the street and covered their "Casa Loco" guesthouse. If you're looking for a Mexican-themed creative getaway in Tampa Bay, you won't find a more memorable place to stay.

In addition to the visual artists you'll find there, you can also catch Grammy Award winning musicians, open mic performances, and a variety of other events listed on their website at www.shamc.org.

Be sure to get a picture with Flower Power Ellie, SHAMc's psychedelic pink painted pachyderm mascot.

Focused as they are on community, Kiaralinda and Ramquist more recently took on an even larger-scale endeavor, transforming the former Rigsby House into the Safety Harbor Art and Music Center (SHAMc). Within its shimmering, mirrored mosaic exterior, SHAMc offers a variety of classes and original works by local artists.

ONE PIECE AT A TIME

What: Whimzeyland and the Safety Harbor Art and Music Center

Where: 1206 Third St. N., Safety Harbor (Whimzeyland) and 706 Second St. N., Safety Harbor (SHAMc)

Cost: Free; donations are appreciated.

Pro Tip: If you want to get involved with and/or support local arts through SHAMc, you can always call 727.725.4018 for more information.

A WING AND A PRAYER

What accidental architectural feature has helped make the Church by the Sea famous?

For more than 70 years now, the Church by the Sea has been meeting the spiritual needs within and beyond Treasure Island, Madeira Beach, and St. Pete Beach. Since 1944, the church has served its fair share of snowbirds, but there's one bird that seems to have nested there permanently.

The building's stained-glass artwork is, similarly, a blend of oceanic images and religious iconography. The original pulpit and altar fixtures, as well as the baptismal font that is still currently in use, were the handiwork of the church's founding pastor and carpenter, Reverend Philip H. Ralph. While all of these architectural elements are interesting, it's the Spanish-style tower with circular windows at the center of the church which invariably receives the most attention, due to a distinctive and loveable architectural anomaly: its unmistakable resemblance to a chicken perched atop the building.

HOUSES OF THE HOLY

What: The Church by the Sea

Where: 495 137th Avenue Cir., Madeira Beach

Cost: Free

Pro Tip: If you visit, please be respectful.

If you're looking for other unique and unusual religious sites, you can also explore Koreshan State Park, which was once home to a utopian colony based on a variant of the Hollow Earth concept.

Atop the Church by the Sea is what may be Florida's most adorable architectural oddity.

For years, a light atop the tower served as a beacon and nautical landmark for local fisherman. The 25-foot mast and beacon made it, for a time, the tallest building in town. The original beacon has since been replaced by a lighted cross. If it's true that the lord works in mysterious ways, perhaps the inadvertently fowl-shaped tower is part of some greater plan to invite curiosity seekers into the flock.

SOURCES

The Story of Tampa: https://www.tampagov.net/art-programs/Info/story-of-tampa

The Most Celebrated Pirate Who Probably Never Lived: https://en.wikipedia.org/wiki/Jos%C3%A9_Gaspar; https://www.atlasobscura.com/places/gasparilla-pirate-festival

City Within a City Delving Deeper Into Ybor: https://yborcityonline.com; Hare, Kristen. 100 Things to do in Tampa Bay Before You Die (Second Edition). St. Louis, MO. Reedy Press, 2018; https://patch.com/florida/southtampa/visit-these-sites-if-you-dare-tampas-most-haunted-places

Florida's First Magic Kingdom: https://www.ut.edu/about-ut/henry-b-plant-museum; https://www.atlasobscura.com/places/henry-b-plant-museum

Extra Credit: https://www.roadsideamerica.com/story/14158; https://www.atlasobscura.com/places/gravity-research-foundation-monument-university-of-tampa

Cracker Country: http://www.crackercountry.org

Shine On: https://stpeteartsalliance.org/shine-mural-festival

Rooftop Oddities: https://www.atlasobscura.com/places/odyssey-2001-spaceship; https://www.roadsideamerica.com/tip/28258

Shelter From the Storm: Muncy, Mark and Schultz, Kari. Freaky Florida. Charleston, SC. The History Press, 2018

Purveyors of the Peculiar: https://www.atlasobscura.com/places/dysfunctional-grace-art-co

Visions of Kerouac: https://www.tampabay.com/arts-entertainment/arts/books/2019/10/22/jack-kerouac-found-the-end-of-his-road-in-st-petersburg-50-years-ago

Gardens Gone Wild: https://www.roadsideamerica.com/tip/298; http://www.stpete.org/attractions/sunken_gardens/index.php

Safety Harbor's Oldest Resident: https://jessicaotoole.com/the-baranoff-oak

A Major League Collection: http://www.littlecooperstown.com/Home_Page.html; https://www.roadsideamerica.com/story/41779

Foreign Soil: https://www.atlasobscura.com/places/parque-amigos-de-jose-marti

Hooked on Live Mermaid Shows: Clark, James C. Hidden History of Florida. Charleston, SC. The History Press, 2015

Roughing It: https://tamparoughriders.org/page-18212

Victory is Ours: http://www.americanvictory.org; https://www.roadsideamerica.com/tip/45469

Strawberry Fields Forever: https://flstrawberryfestival.com/history

The Hand of Fate: https://www.tampabay.com/news/humaninterest/memorial-to-fishermen-lost-at-sea-unveiled-in-madeira-beach/1227667

Branching Out: https://photos.cltampa.com/remembering-the-legendary-kapok-tree-inn-floridas-most-insane-restaurant/?slide=1&com07121

South by Southwest: https://www.atlasobscura.com/places/james-museum-of-western-wildlife-art

Almost Famous: Schmit, Brian. Glory Days, The History of New Port Richey Florida. New Port Richey, FL. Yankee Doodle Press, LLC, 2017

A Sunny Place for Shady People: Deitche, Scott M. Cigar City Mafia: A Complete History of the Tampa Underworld. Barricade Books, 2005

The Mother of All Specialty Museums: https://mommuseum.org/tag/st-petersburg-florida

A Cut Above the Rest: https://bernssteakhouse.com/our-story

A Deep Dive Into Tarpon Springs: https://www.atlasobscura.com/places/tarpon-springs-epiphany-celebration; https://www.atlasobscura.com/places/spongeorama-sponge-factory

The Greatest Show on Earth: https://www.ringling.org/history-ringling

On the Rocks: https://www.gq.com/story/john-susor-nine-wives-serial-husband-200704; https://www.legacy.com/obituaries/TampaBayTimes/obituary.aspx?page=lifestory&pid=101346712

Triassic Park: https://www.roadsideamerica.com/tip/295

Against the Grain: http://sandingovationsmasterscup.com

That's How We Roll: https://tabanerocigars.com/blogs/tabanero-blog/the-history-of-the-tampa-cigar-industry

Beachfront Surreal Estate: https://thedali.org/about-the-museum

Blood and Gold: https://en.wikipedia.org/wiki/P%C3%A1nfilo_de_Narv%C3%A1ez; https://www.atlasobscura.com/places/jungle-prada-site

Pirates, Politicians, and Pioneer Priests: Bender, Shelby Jean Robertson and Dunham, Elizabeth Laramie. Images of America Tampa's Historic Cemeteries. Charleston, SC. Arcadia Publishing, 2013

Upcycled: https://patch.com/florida/templeterrace/business-profile-the-story-behind-the-eye-catching-arb86d1ce777

City in a Sandwich: https://en.wikipedia.org/wiki/Cuban_sandwich

Down the Rabbit Hole: https://www.rabbitholeescapegames.com

The Gulp Coast: https://www.visitstpeteclearwater.com/gulp-coast-craft-beer-trail?gclid=EAlaIQobChMI3NmMz8aL6gIVl4TICh0E7QBuEAAYASAAEgK9CPD_BwE#block-vspc-itineraries-itinerary-list-1?

Glass Wizardry: https://www.atlasobscura.com/places/chihuly-collection

Cinema Paradiso: https://www.atlasobscura.com/places/tampa-theatre

Winter's Tail: https://www.seewinter.com/winter-and-hope/winter

Every Day I'm Shuffling: https://stpeteshuffle.com/history.html

The Legendary Pink Palace: Hurley Young, June. The Don Ce-Sar Story. St. Petersburg, FL. Partnership Press, 2007

The Other British Invasion of Florida: https://www.facebook.com/PENNY-LANE-Beatles-Museum-1107244892687449

A Burning Question: Carlson, Charlie. Weird Florida. Toronto, Ontario, Canada. Sterling Publishing Co., Inc. 2005

One of Us! One of Us!: https://www.theguardian.com/us-news/2015/feb/26/welcome-to-gibtown-the-last-freakshow-town-in-america; https://en.wikipedia.org/wiki/Gibsonton,_Florida; https://www.atlasobscura.com/places/gibsonton-florida

The Warlock of Wesley Chapel: https://www.facebook.com/notes/the-warlock-house-enchantment-vandercar-studios/biography-of-lewis-vandercar/432591413464096

They Paved Paradise and Put up a Parking Lot: http://designandtime.com/we/blog/?p=1711

Can I get an Amen?: https://www.roadsideamerica.com/story/14159

Left for Dead: https://en.wikipedia.org/wiki/Dade_massacre

Form and Function: https://urbanlegendsofflorida.homestead.com/

The Biggest Little Train in Tampa Bay: http://www.lcrailroad.org/

Buried Treasure: http://www.mulberryphosphatemuseum.org/aboutus.html

Where the Sidewalk (Never) Ends: https://en.wikipedia.org/wiki/Bayshore_Boulevard

Sea Cow Sanctuary: https://www.tampaelectric.com/company/mvc; https://www.atlasobscura.com/places/manatee-viewing-area

The Birthplace of Death Metal: https://www.revolvermag.com/music/florida-death-metals-gory-rise-groundbreaking-reign-definitive-oral-history; http://morrisound.com/about

Blessed Be the Windows of the Seminole Finance Company: https://www.atlasobscura.com/places/clearwater-virgin-mary

Braden Castle Ruins: https://www.atlasobscura.com/places/braden-castle-ruins

Bodies in Motion: https://www.themovementsanctuary.com

Children of the Sun: https://www.flsouthern.edu/frank-lloyd-wright/home.aspx; https://www.atlasobscura.com/places/child-of-the-sun-campus

Flotsam and Jetsam: https://seahagg.com; https://www.youtube.com/watch?v=dJT02fNdGml

Forget Not Thy Beach Towel, Ezekiel: https://www.atlasobscura.com/places/pinecraft; https://www.sarasotamagazine.com/news-and-profiles/2018/04/tourist-pinecraft-sarasota

A Doubleheader in Seminole Heights: https://www.atlasobscura.com/places/twoheaded-gator-of-seminole-heights; https://www.tampabay.com/news/humaninterest/its-a-total-crock/2186639/

Tampa's Restaurant Royalty: https://www.columbiarestaurant.com/The-Columbia-Experience/History

Use Well These Few but Ever Fleeting Hours: http://www.williamculbertson.com/tampa-centennial-keep.html; https://www.fox13news.com/news/memorial-functions-as-a-sundial-tells-story-of-9-11

A Towering Enigma: https://en.wikipedia.org/wiki/Sulphur_Springs_Water_Tower

Dead Men Tell Tall Tales: https://www.atlasobscura.com/places/grave-of-americas-oldest-man

Molly the Mollusk: https://www.atlasobscura.com/places/molly-the-mollusk

Castle in the Swamp: http://solomonscastle.com; https://www.atlasobscura.com/places/solomons-castle

From Hard Luck to Hard Rock: https://seminoletribune.org/hard-rock-tampa-celebrates-10-years

Steam Engines of War: Cerf, Alain A. Nicholas Cugnot and the Chariot of Fire. St. Petersburg, FL. Tampa Bay Automobile Museum, 2010; https://www.atlasobscura.com/places/fardier-de-cugnot-tampa-bay-automobile-museum

Small Wonder: https://www.tampapix.com/snowpark.htm

Play It Again: https://www.replaymuseum.org/

Juiced: https://www.boyettsgrove.com; https://www.roadsideamerica.com/tip/8201

Bridge over Troubled Water: https://www.wtsp.com/article/news/history/remembering-the-sunshine-skyway-bridge-collapse-40-years-later/67-a33b0ec1-7184-4065-8c53-c23cfe05488e

The Lost Cemeteries of Hillsborough: http://www.thafl.com/Zion/Default.aspx

An Island in the Sun: http://egmontkey.info/page-1717533

Tiny Terrors: https://www.tampabay.com/features/humaninterest/have-you-seen-the-mini-lights-haunting-st-pete-these-people-have/2300409; https://www.cltampa.com/arts-entertainment/culture/article/20977632/mini-lights-an-evolving-urban-legend

Creative Transformation: http://www.whimsymuseum.org/id25.html

For Whom the Bells Toll: https://boktowergardens.org/our-history

More than Just a Whim: http://www.safetyharborartandmusiccenter.com; https://www.atlasobscura.com/places/whimzeyland

A Wing and a Prayer: https://www.churchbythesea.com/about-1

INDEX